ARTS AND THE STATES

A Report of the
ARTS TASK FORCE
NATIONAL CONFERENCE OF STATE LEGISLATURES

Compiled by Larry Briskin

National Conference of State Legislatures
Earl S. Mackey, Executive Director
Deborah E.S. Bennington, Senior Manager
Arts and the States Project

Copyright 1981 by National Conference of State Legislatures

Library of Congress Catalog Card Number: 81-82925

ISBN 0-941336-00-X

Designed by:
The Tsuruda Group, Sacramento, California

Typography by:
Off/Setters, West Sacramento, California in Megaron medium and bold

Printing by:
Fong & Fong, Sacramento, California

Additional copies of Arts and the States *may be ordered at $6.00 per copy from:*

National Conference of State Legislatures
1125 17th Street, 15th Floor
Denver, Colorado 80202

Photo Credits

4 — Jan Bauman, Mill Valley, California
8 — *Right* — Donald Coy, Fox Studios, Santa Monica, California
9 — *Left* — Steven Hunt, Utah Arts Council
9 — *Center* — Bruce Boehner, Los Angeles
13 — Kingsbury Studios, Portsmouth, New Hampshire
17 — M. Florian
20 — *Left* — Gail Bryan
20 — *Right Center* — Bruce Baker, Utah Arts Council
25 — *Left* — eeva-inkeri, New York City
25 — *Right* — Pach Brothers, New York City
43 — *Top* — Margaret Bauman, Fairbanks, Alaska
45 — Steven Hunt, Utah Arts Council
46 — Teri Slotkin, CETA Artists Project, Brooklyn
52 — Audrey Tsuruda, Sacramento, California
55 — *Left* — Ken Howard, New York City
55 — *Right* — Susan Cook, New York City
58 — Bonnie Tiegel — Los Angeles
61 — Harold Briskin, Palm Springs
69 — *Right* — Marianne Barcellona, New York City
73 — Tracey Landworth, Los Angeles
83 — *Center* — Marbeth, New York City
83 — *Right* — Bruce Baker, Utah Arts Council
92 — *Center* — Martha Swope, New York City
92 — *Right* — Teri Slotkin, CETA Artists Project, Brooklyn

TABLE OF CONTENTS

The more than 60 state legislators who served on the NCSL's Arts Task Force are pleased to present this report on state support for the arts to our fellow legislators and to the public.

The National Conference of State Legislatures established the Arts Task Force in July, 1978, by inviting each state to appoint one or more members. From the Task Force's inception, its members demonstrated great interest and enthusiasm. The nine Task Force meetings were informative, stimulating and enjoyable and are reported to be among the best attended of any group that NCSL has sponsored. Task Force members applied the knowledge gained at these meetings to enact arts legislation, to increase state arts appropriations, and to implement other important arts programs and policies in their home states.

One of the keys to the Task Force's success has been a deliberate structuring of its meetings. In addition to the traditional mode of legislative meetings — speeches, panels, hearings, and discussions — we made a conscious effort to involve the members in direct contact with artists, in actual participation in the arts, as well as in attending arts events. Museums, art galleries, symphony halls, theatres, ballet performances, and schools were all on our agenda, but we also met and talked with artists in the artists' own environment — in their studios, galleries, in rehearsal and teaching space, at theatres and production sites.

Some of the highlights of our meetings, which I believe exemplify this process, are these:

- In Los Angeles, after attending a performance of "Zoot Suit," we met with director Gordon Davidson and members of the cast to discuss the play, theatre company operations, and issues raised by the actors.

  At the home of Frederick and Marcia Weisman, surrounded by their beautiful contemporary art collection, we engaged in a sometimes heated exchange between visual artists and legislators over how state government can advance the rights of visual artists.

- In Santa Fe, we learned about historic preservation through both a slide presentation and a walking tour of restored buildings.

  We met and discussed artists' needs with Native American artists and craftsmen at the Institute of American Indian Art.

- In New York, we were treated to an exhilarating studio performance by the Dance Theatre of Harlem. Director Arthur Mitchell spoke about the difficulties of funding scholarships for disadvantaged youth and his success in instilling a sense of accomplishment and self-esteem in so many young people.

  We toured the SoHo district, talked with artists, and discussed the issues of live-work space.

  We learned about ballet firsthand by actually taking a lesson at the Eliot Feld Ballet School.

  We visited Lincoln Center and the Lincoln Center Institute, learning about in-service arts education teacher training.

- In New Orleans (as well as in Los Angeles), we listened to jazz and talked with the musicians about how legislators could assist the training of young musicians and address the question of high unemployment in the music field.

  We visited the New Orleans Center for the Creative Arts, a public arts high school, and talked with arts educators, artists, and students.

- In Nashville, we not only had a panel discussion on crafts featuring some of the nation's most knowledgeable people, but also visited with some of America's next generation of craftspeople training at the new Appalachian Crafts Center.

  We visited a recording studio, during which the members experienced record and tape production and talked with producers and manufacturers about recording industry problems.

- None of the members will forget the

excitement of meeting with opera composer Gian Carlo Menotti in Charleston, South Carolina and talking with him about opera, art, and festivals.

It has also been a process of learning from each other and of sharing experiences — a process that has created strong friendships and a sense of community among the Task Force members.

The meetings have given us a sense of commitment and direction that is set forth in the NCSL Policy Resolution on the Arts, recommended by the Arts Task Force and adopted by the NCSL, and in the Task Force's recommended legislation. Already, in almost every state, Arts Task Force members are suggesting and passing some of these bills.

We hope that this process will be carried forward to others through this report. *Arts and the States* will be successful if it aids other state legislators in identifying areas of interest and in focusing their efforts to support the arts at the state level.

We are extremely pleased that the NCSL Executive Committee recognized arts and culture as an important state concern for the future and, effective in February, 1981, created the Arts and the States Committee as part of the NCSL's Assembly on the Legislature. Chaired by Maine Representative Merle Nelson, an original Task Force member, the Committee will extend and expand the Task Force's work as part of the continuing NCSL structure.

Acknowledgements

There are many whom we wish to thank for their valuable contributions to the Task Force's work and to this report's production. We extend our appreciation:

To NCSL Project Director Deborah Bennington, for her tremendous talent and continuing dedication to the Arts and the States Project.

To Larry Briskin, my former administrative assistant, who was invaluable in implementing the Task Force programs and who compiled and wrote a major portion of this publication.

To NCSL Presidents George Roberts, Jason Boe, and Richard Hodes, and the NCSL Executive Committee and staff for their strong support of the Arts Task Force.

To the National Endowment for the Arts, and to Chairman Livingston Biddle and Partnership Director Hank Putsch, for the $25,000 in seed funding that made possible creation of the Arts Task Force.

To the corporations, corporate foundations, other organizations and individuals whose contributions have supported the production and printing of this report.

To the arts administrators in the many states we visited, to their staffs, and to the many local participants who made our meetings so stimulating and productive. Special thanks are due to Bernie Lopez (Santa Fe), Kitty Carlisle Hart and David Mendoza (New York), Al Head (New Orleans), Ed Harrison (Denver), Ellen Dressler (Charleston), Art Keeble (Nashville), Frank Cooper (Miami), and Wayne Lawson (Columbus); and to Bill Eels, Roy Helms, Paul Hollrah, Ralph Loomis, and Bennett Tarleton, for their faithful involvement and support.

To Sam Francis, for creating the beautiful art that appears on our cover and for allowing us to use it. Thanks also to Hugh Levin of the Harry N. Abrams Company for his cooperation.

To those who volunteered to write a portion of this report: Minnesota Senator Emily Anne Staples (Historic Preservation), Roy Helms, Lani Lattin Duke, Arley Curtz and Jim Andrews (who wrote about methods used to increase arts appropriations in their states); Romalyn Tilghman (Community Arts Agencies and Rural Areas and the Arts); Alan Jabbour (Folk Arts); and Mary Brabston (Arts and the Disabled).

To the staff and interns who conducted research and aided in the writing and production of this report: Joan Smith, Paula Olson, Eileen Moran, Marilyn Riley, Sharon Gold, Margaret McMurray, Michael Styles, Robert Glasser, Debora Chan, and Bob Jones.

To my Task Force colleagues for their interest, support, and warm friendship. It has been a rare privilege and wonderful experience working with you in this labor of love.

And finally, a special note of thanks to Rubin Gorewitz, founder and president of Artists Rights Today, Inc., for inspiring us and for always being there when we needed him.

California State Senator Alan Sieroty Chairman, NCSL Arts Task Force

THE NCSL AND THE ARTS

"I believe that every government has a moral obligation to support creative expression which ultimately becomes reflected in some art form. It follows that government support for the arts is natural, normal and essential in a free society."

Maine Representative Merle Nelson Chair, Arts and the States Committee

The performing, visual and literary arts are an essential element of the quality of life in every state, a means of creative expression for artists, and a source of enjoyment for all. Accessibility to the arts should be provided to every individual.

Citizen demand for arts experiences has generated greater public and private support for the arts, creating a beneficial cultural impact on the community.

State legislatures have a continuing interest in the availability of the arts and should encourage coordinated efforts among all levels of government fostering the arts.

State legislatures can act to ensure an environment conducive to the freedom of artistic expression, enabling the arts to contribute greatly to our cultural, educational and economic well-being.

The National Conference of State Legislatures encourages state legislatures to pursue policies which:

● Place increased emphasis on appropriations for the arts and for state arts agency programs to make the arts accessible to all citizens.[1]

● Give greater recognition to the creativity of artists and protect artists' rights through appropriate legislation.[2]

● Preserve the rich, multi-cultural artistic, architectural, and historic heritage of our nation.[3]

● Exert leadership to stimulate the support which corporations, foundations, other public interest organizations, and private citizens provide for arts activities.

● Provide funds to integrate art into the design, construction, and renovation of state buildings.[4]

● Encourage the improvement of arts education programs for students and teachers, and the integration of the arts into the education curriculum.[5]

● Encourage legislative recognition of the importance of the arts and cultural activities by providing a forum for legislative action relating to the arts.[6]

● Educate the community on the economic benefits of the arts.[7]

● Utilize the arts in programs for youth, the aging, the disabled, neighborhood, community, and rural development, transportation, and the prevention of crime and delinquency.[8]

● Encourage the sharing of arts resources and information among states.[9]

NOTES:

1. See *State Arts Agencies*, pages 84-87; *Percent-for-Art in Public Places*, pages 16-24; *The Arts in Education*, pages 16-24; *State Governmental Organization of the Arts*, pages 41-42; *Art Banks*, pages 43-44; and *Artists-in-Residence*, pages 45-46.

2. See *Artists' Rights*, pages 25-33; *Percent-For-Art in Public Places*, pages 12-15; *Art Banks*, pages 43-44.

3. See *Art Preservation*, pages 30-31; *Historic Preservation*, pages 49-50; *Minorities and the Arts*, pages 91-92.

4. See *Percent-For-Art in Public Places*, pages 12-15.

5. See *The Arts in Education*, pages 16-24; *Artists-in-Residence*, pages 45-46.

6. See *Giving the Arts Importance Within the State Legislative Structure*, pages 72-73.

7. See *The Economic Impact Approach*, pages 56-58.

8. See *Arts and the Disabled*, pages 92-93; *Rural Areas and the Arts*, pages 88-89; *Community Arts Agencies*, pages 87-88; *Minorities and the Arts*, pages 91-92; *The Economic Impact Approach*, pages 56-58; and *The Arts' Healing Role*, pages 93-94.

9. See the *Chairman's Introduction*, pages 4-5.

At its July, 1979 Annual Meeting, upon recommendation of its Arts Task Force, the National Conference of State Legislatures adopted the above policy resolution on "Public Support for the Arts." (The policy recommendations are cross-referenced by footnote to sections of this report.)

SUMMARY OF RECOMMENDED STATE ARTS LEGISLATION

The Arts Task Force has adopted the following as recommended state action for the arts. The Task Force recognizes that not every proposal may be suitable for enactment in every state.

PERCENT-FOR-ART IN PUBLIC PLACES

Percent-for-Art in Public Places: Appropriate a specific percentage, often 1%, of the annual construction budget for state buildings to commission, and/or purchase art for new and existing state buildings; or, less preferably, require legislative consideration of annual or specific appropriations to commission and/or purchase art for these buildings.

THE ARTS IN EDUCATION

Basic Education: Amend the state education act to redefine basic education to include arts education at the elementary and secondary levels.

In-Service Teacher Training: Make state funds available to interested school districts to provide in-service arts education training for elementary school teachers. Training programs should emphasize both arts experiences and appreciation, and integration of the arts into the educational curriculum as a means of teaching math, reading, science, and other basic subjects.

Gifted and Talented: Include children gifted and talented in the arts within categorical state funding of gifted and talented programs.

Schools for the Arts: Consider funding schools for the arts to provide intensive training opportunities for artistically gifted

and talented school-age children. The schools may be organized as (1) summer schools for the arts, (2) schools where a substantial portion of the day is devoted to arts instruction, or (3) after-school arts instruction programs.

ARTISTS' RIGHTS

Artist-Art Dealer Relations: Provide protection to artists who give their works to art dealers on consignment to sell or exhibit. The dealer acts as a trustee in holding the art and funds from sales. Some laws also protect artists against loss or damage to the artworks while in the dealers' possession and against claims by dealers' creditors.

Artists' Live-Work Space: Allow local governments to establish zones where artists may live and work in buildings in urban areas previously zoned for commercial and/or industrial use and to authorize alternative building code requirements in those areas.

Art Preservation: Provide artists, and in some cases the public, the right to bring legal action against intentional physical defacement, alteration, or destruction by government agencies or private owners of artworks of recognized quality. Both injunctive relief and action for damages may be authorized. Sometimes referred to as "Artists' Moral Rights."

Resale Royalties: Provide artists with a percentage of the resale price of their artworks, provided that the resale is profitable to the seller and the resale price is in excess of a specific minimum amount.

TAX LEGISLATION

Artists' Income Tax Deductions: Enable professional artists, for state income tax purposes, to deduct the fair market value of artworks they create and donate to museums and other charitable organizations. Current law limits the artists' tax deduction to the cost of materials.

Death Taxes: (1) Allow beneficiaries of artists' estates to defer death taxes, and/or (2) allow the death tax to be paid with art as valued by the state death tax appraiser and delivered to an appropriate institution.

CONSUMER PROTECTION FOR PURCHASERS OF ART

Disclosure: Protect purchasers of fine art prints and other art issued in limited editions by requiring art dealers to disclose specific information regarding each piece sold.

Warranties: Require art dealers to provide express warranties of genuineness with respect to the sale of limited edition prints and other artworks.

STATE GOVERNMENTAL ORGANIZATION OF THE ARTS

Department of Cultural Resources: Consider the feasibility and advisability of creating a state department to administer programs that may include some or all of the following: state culture, arts, library, tourism, and humanities agencies. Some states may place the department secretary or director on the governor's cabinet. Where a state department is not feasible or advisable, program coordination among the various agencies should be encouraged.

Composition of State Arts Agencies: Consider the feasibility and advisability of requiring one or more professional visual, literary, or performing artists on the state arts council or commission.

OTHER ISSUES

Art Banks: Establish a state art bank through which the state, with the help of experts, purchases artwork by the state's artists to rent or loan for public display in public and private nonprofit facilities. Rental fees are used to purchase new art and for administrative expenses.

Artists-in-Residence: Establish artists-in-residence programs for such institutions as schools, hospitals, and prisons.

Direct Appropriations for Arts Institutions: Consider direct appropriations to major arts institutions either for specific capital expenditures or to provide a significant portion of the institution's budget. Such appropriations are in addition to the regular funding of the state arts agency.

Historic Preservation: Encourage legislation to provide both incentives and funding for the preservation of landmarks and properties that possess artistic, cultural, historic, or architectural significance.

Nonprofit Arts Organizations: Simplify initial applications and annual reporting requirements for small arts organizations filing for state nonprofit, tax-exempt status.

Local Arts Funding: (1) Allow local governments to institute a hotel-motel tax or other taxes to fund cultural and tourism-related institutions and events. (2) Authorize local governments to provide funding for arts performances such as operas, symphonies, concerts, theatre, and dance, for art exhibitions, and for a percent-for-art program for local public buildings and facilities.

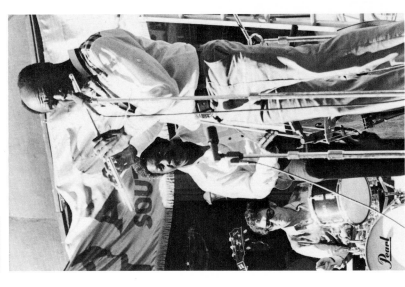

Jazz musician Buddy Collette (right) and his group played at the Task Force's Los Angeles meeting and talked with members about how legislators could assist the training of young musicians.

RECOMMENDED STATE ARTS LEGISLATION

The late 1970's saw legislators in almost every state successfully authoring bills affecting the arts. The chart on the following pages shows the arts-related laws that have been passed by each state.

Rapid expansion in this legislative area is the result of individual legislators' interest in the arts, public approval of allocating tax dollars to support the arts, and energetic advocacy efforts by artists, arts organizations, and statewide arts advocacy groups. From the initial Arts Task Force meeting in November, 1978, members determined that recommending state arts legislation would be among their most important tasks.

The Arts Task Force adopted 21 recommendations over the course of three meetings — in San Francisco in July, 1979, in Charleston, South Carolina in May, 1980, and in New York City in July, 1980.

The format for presenting the recommendations includes a general discussion, analysis of the laws of states that have adopted that recommendation, supporting points, and, in many cases, other important considerations for legislators proposing the recommendation.

Percent-for-art in public places and arts education are the recommendations to which the Task Force has given the highest priority.

The order of the remaining recommendations is not intended to indicate priorities. The Task Force recognizes that not every proposal may be suitable for enactment by every state.

is parent/child dance class in Utah exemplifies the
ortant role the arts play in developing children's
ativity, expression of feeling, and sense of beauty.
e The Arts in Education, page 16)

The Bradbury Building in Los Angeles illustrates how restored buildings with historic, cultural and architectural significance can preserve our heritage for future generations. (See Historic Preservation, page 49.)

Art-in-Public-Places and Percent-for-Art programs bring art out of museums and into people's lives. Bruce Beasley's "Apolymon" adorns two adjacent state buildings in Sacramento, California. (See Percent-for-Art in Public Places, page 12.)

SURVEY
OF
STATE
ARTS
LEGISLATION

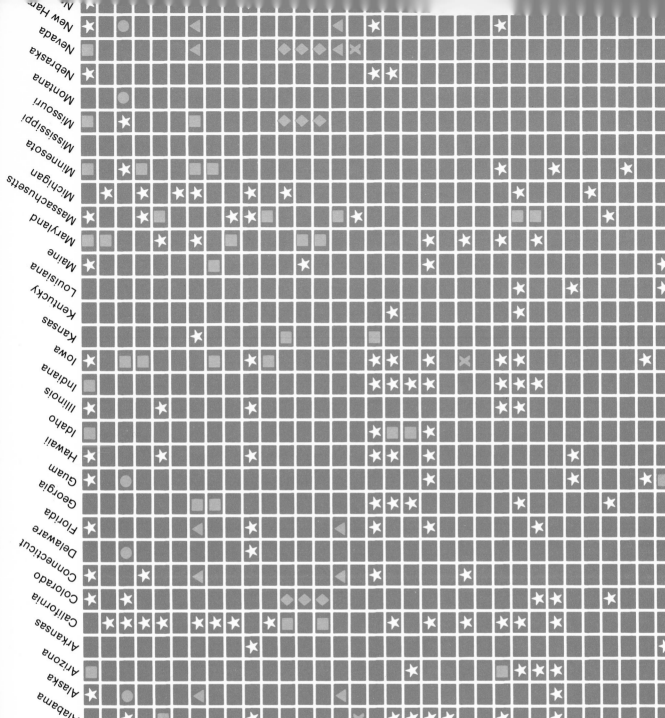

EXPLANATION OF SYMBOLS

Symbol	Meaning
★	Legislation Enacted
■	Legislation Introduced but not Enacted
◀	No State Income Tax
●	No State Sales Tax
◆	No State Death Tax
✕	Prohibited by State Constitution or Statute

	New York	North Carolina	North Dakota	Ohio	Oklahoma	Oregon	Pennsylvania	Puerto Rico	Rhode Island	South Carolina	South Dakota	Tennessee	Texas	Utah	Vermont	Virginia	Washington	West Virginia	Wisconsin	Wyoming	No. of States That Have Enacted Law Before 12/31/80
Percent for Art in State Buildings	■	■				★	■				■	■	★	■	■		★		★	■	17
Annual Appropriation for Art in State Buildings											★										3
;ales and Use Tax Exemption for Museum Purchases	★	★		■		●											■				7
Artist-Art Dealer Relations Act	★			■			■					■	★				■		★		8
Disclosure of Info to Purchasers of Art	★			■								■	■								5
Warranties of Genuineness	★											■	■								2
Artists' Fair Market Value Income Tax Deduction	■				■	★				★	▲	▲					▲			▲	6
Resale Royalties	■			■			■					■	■								1
Artists' Live-Work Space: Local Authorization	★	★																			4
Direct Appropriations for Arts Institutions	★	★			★		★	★	★			★		★		★	★				20
Art Preservation (Moral Rights)						■						■					■				1
Deferral of Death Taxes for Artists' Heirs															◆						1
Pay Death Tax with Art															◆						1
Value Art at Cost of Materials-Death Taxes						■									◆						0
Income Tax Check-off To Benefit the Arts	■					■	■				▲	▲					▲			▲	0
State Lottery for the Arts																					1
Define Basic Education to Include Arts Education	★					★				★							★		★		15
Education Training Required for Teacher Certification[2]		★	★		★							★		★							13
In-Service Arts Education Training[2]			★											★			★				7
Gifted and Talented Programs Include the Arts[2]	★					★	■			★							★				15
State School for the Arts[2]	★	★			★		★			★						■					7
osition of State Arts Agencies: Legislative Representation	■			★			★										★				6
position of State Arts Agencies: Artist Representation	■													★							1
Authorizes County Arts Funding	★			★			★							★			★	★			15
Authorizes Local Hotel-Motel Occupancy Tax													★	★		★	★				14
Authorizes Other Taxes for Local Arts Funding																★		★			7
lates Authenticity of Native American Arts and Crafts					★						★						■				9
Standing Legislative Arts Committee	★	★																			3
Joint Legislative Arts Committee																	★				2
Select or Special Legislative Arts Committee	★																				4
Legislative Subcommittee on the Arts						★													★		3
Legislative Task Force on the Arts										★											3
)epartment Structure for State Cultural Agencies		★						★			★						■	★			7

}esolution passed in 1980 — Tennessee Arts Commission will submit

states accomplish this by legislation, others by state education
nt or other state agency regulations.

RECOMMENDATION:

Appropriate a specific percentage, often 1%, of the annual construction budget for state buildings to commission and/or purchase art for new and existing state buildings; or, less preferably, require legislative consideration of annual or specific appropriations to commission and/or purchase art for these buildings.

The Arts Task Force recommends percent-for-art in public places as one of the highest priorities for state legislative action in the arts.

Beginning with Hawaii in 1967, nineteen states and Guam have enacted percent-for-art or art-in-state-buildings statutes aimed at beautifying state-funded structures.[1] The federal government (through administrative regulations) and many local communities

"Art in public places enlivens, enhances, and enriches those spaces that otherwise would remain cold and monotonous. It celebrates 'today' by using contemporary artists and, as a mirror of society, reflects the complicated, all encompassing, fragmented, innovative, joyous strength and sorrow of the age. And, for the first time in many years, it brings the professional artist and architect back together. Art in public places brings art out of our museums and into our schools, buildings, parks, malls, and, most importantly, into our lives."
— Oregon State Senator Richard Bullock

have also established such programs. This action is a recognition that the sterile, functional architecture that has long dominated government construction is outmoded and that today Americans want environments filled with beauty and grace. Percent-for-art is a complex legislative issue. As the chart on page 14 indicates, state laws vary widely and embody different approaches to achieve common goals. Among the many questions that should be carefully considered by the legislature are:

WHAT PERCENTAGE OF THE BUDGET SHOULD BE ALLOCATED? HOW IS IT TO BE CALCULATED? IS IT A MINIMUM OR A MAXIMUM? MANDATORY OR OPTIONAL?

Most state statutes specify 1%; some indicate not less than 1%, and others, not more than that amount. Maine allocates the lesser of 1% or $25,000. Thus for any building costing more than $2.5 million, the amount for art will be less than 1%.

All but five of the state statutes mandate a specified percentage. California's experience with a non-mandatory law illustrates the problems with this approach. California's statute requires the governor to include an appropriation for art in state buildings in the annual budget bill, which is subject to legislative approval. Since the program began in 1977, the governor's four recommendations have ranged from $300,000 to $1.4 million. With one exception, the legislature has reduced the recommended amount, and once it was eliminated entirely. **The Arts Task Force urges states to enact percent-for-art measures that establish a fixed or a minimum mandatory percentage.**

calculate the percent-for-art figure for each building. However, several specify that the amount be based on actual construction costs and not include planning, land acquisition, site work, or other non-construction expenditures. States vary as to whether to include in the percent-for-art base such capital outlay items as prisons, highways, warehouses, and remodeling projects.

WHICH BUILDINGS SHOULD HAVE ART? SHOULD APPROPRIATIONS BE SPENT ON SPECIFIC BUILDINGS OR SHOULD THEY BE POOLED?

Many state laws either do not address the issue of eligible buildings or delegate its determination to an administrative agency. In addition to new buildings, each state should decide whether to provide art for existing state buildings.

The choice between specific allocations or pooling is an important issue. The former ensures that each eligible building receives art proportional to its cost, while the latter provides flexibility and may result in enhancement of existing state buildings or other public places.

Oregon's 1976-79 program illustrates the pooling approach. With a $96,115 budget accumulated under a flexible, mandatory 1% statute, a public collection of 170 artworks in various media was acquired for public display in and around the Salem State Capitol Mall. The art represents 145 artists and craftspeople, 120 of whom live in the state.

WHO ADMINISTERS THE PROGRAM? SHOULD ADMINISTRATIVE COSTS BE DEDUCTED FROM THE PERCENTAGE APPROPRIATION?

Most statutes ignore the question of how to

Choosing the appropriate administrative agency is important. Which agency is suitable depends on each state's governmental organization and the administrative capabilities of particular administrative agencies. All but two states involve the state arts agency.

The source of administrative costs is a thorny problem. Reducing the amount available for art in order to pay for administration will not be popular, but proper administration is essential to the program's professionalism and ultimate success. Provision should be made for administration, either as a portion of the available funding or separately in the administering agency's budget. New Hampshire, the only state that limits administrative costs, provides a maximum 8% of the program money for implementation.

WHAT IS THE SELECTION PROCESS FOR COMMISSIONING ARTISTS OR PURCHASING ART, AND WHO MAKES THE DECISIONS?

Probably the most difficult issue is the selection process. How and by whom the selection is made ultimately affects the quality of the art and its public acceptance. Open competition is the most democratic

method but also administratively the most expensive. Commissions limited to a few invited artists or direct commissioning of a specific artist are more manageable but may include only "name" artists and limit opportunities for other deserving individuals. Direct purchase reduces program costs considerably and provides finished art for immediate display, but this approach has several drawbacks. The artist and architect do not work together to achieve artistic and architectural compatibility; the artist loses the opportunity to create art that is responsive to the particular environment; and the purchased art will perhaps not be integrated into the building structure, or, if integrated, may result in additional costs for building modifications, such as resurfacing walls.

Most states appoint advisory committees or juries to make selections. Those bodies either make final decisions or present recommendations to another panel for final determination. Although membership and selection procedures vary widely from state to state, the selection committee generally consists of three to seven members among whom may be the building architect, arts professionals, non-competing artists, building users or other public representatives, and representatives from the resident or contracting agencies and from the state arts agency. To improve chances of the art's favorable public acceptance, the local citizenry and building employees should be involved in the selection process and the art should be highly publicized before placement.

SHOULD THE STATE'S ARTISTS BE GIVEN PREFERENCE FOR

COMMISSIONS? SHOULD COMMISSIONED ARTISTS RETAIN COPYRIGHT AND OTHER INTANGIBLE RIGHTS?

Eleven of the twenty statutes, recognizing that expenditure of state funds is intended to benefit the state's residents, authorize program priority for resident artists. Several extend the preference to former residents, and Nebraska's law offers preference to regional artists. However, this provision has been criticized as parochial, and while it may increase the probability of local acceptance, it tends to exclude artists of national stature.

Four state statutes clearly provide that the state obtains title to the art. Does this provision mean that the artist is prevented from copyrighting his or her creation and that the state has an unlimited right to sell the art but no responsibility to maintain it or prevent its intentional destruction or mutilation? Thus far, only California's and Wisconsin's percent-for-art acts have considered these issues. The Arts Task Force, which has expressed its concern for artists' rights through four recommendations, urges states to consider protecting the intangible rights of artists who are commissioned or whose works are purchased.

FEATURES OF STATE PERCENT-FOR-ART LAWS

This chart reflects statutory provisions enacted through 1980. In many states, administrative agency regulations clarify and supplement the statute.

		Alaska	California	Colorado	Connecticut	Florida	Guam	Hawaii	Illinois	Iowa	Maine	Massachusetts	Michigan	Nebraska	New Hampshire	New Jersey	Oregon	South Dakota	Texas	Washington	Wisconsin
Percentage (U = unspecified)		1	U	1	1	½	1	1	½	½	1	1	1	1	1	1½	1	1	U	1	½ · 2/10
Expenditure Mandatory or Optional	Mandatory	•	•	•		•	•	•	•	•	•	•		•	•	•	•		•	•	•
	Optional				•								•					•			
Administrative Agency	State Arts Agency	•	•	•	•	•		•	•	•	•	•		•	•	•	•	•	•	•	•
	Public Works or General Services Department	•	•	•	•	•	•						•					•		•	
	Finance Department		•			•															
	Other state agency	•					•		•	•					•		•				
	Specifies administrative agency duties	•	•	•		•			•	•		•			•	•	•	•	•	•	•
Buildings Included	New buildings	•	•	•		•	•	•	•	•	•	•	•	•	•	•		•		•	•
	Remodeling projects	•				•	•	•		•		•	•	•	•	•		•		•	
	Existing buildings	•	•																		
	More specific building types named	•	•						•		•				•					•	
	Law applies only when building cost exceeds minimum amount	•					•							•							•
	Excludes specific construction or buildings not designed for public access or use	•	•	•	•	•	•	•		•		•			•	•		•		•	•
Eligible Art	Broad unspecific definition	•																			
	Broad specific definition	•	•		•		•	•	•	•		•		•	•	•		•		•	•
	No definition of art			•																	
	Excludes landscaping, ornaments	•	•			•	•		•	•		•		•	•	•		•		•	•
	Established by statute	•											•							•	
	Established by agency rules		•		•	•		•						•	•		•			•	
	Established by law and agency			•	•					•	•		•	•							
Selection Process	Unspecified																				•
	Selection committee members named	•	•					•		•		•		•	•		•			•	
	Selection process has two or more tiers		•			•	•	•				•		•	•	•			•	•	
	Selection process requires involvement of the public and/or the building occupants	•																			
	Selection committee expenses reimbursed		•					•	•		•				•					•	
	Commissions and purchases	•	•	•		•		•	•	•		•	•	•	•	•		•		•	•
Types of Acquisitions	Commissions only	•			•	•															
	Unspecified			•	•		•	•	•	•						•	•	•	•		•
	State gets title to art		•															•	•	•	
Calculation and Use of Funds	Specifies which project costs are included to calculate amount for art	•	•	•		•		•		•	•		•	•	•		•			•	
	Art funds allocated for a specific building or project	•	•	•		•		•		•				•	•		•		•	•	
	Art funds pooled/may be used for other buildings	•					•						•							•	•
	Private and/or federal funds may be used for art							•									•			•	
Artists	Priority to state's artists	•	•		•			•		•		•	•		•		•	•	•	•	
	Artists retain specific rights																	•		•	
Miscellaneous	Expresses legislative intent	•	•	•	•	•		•	•	•		•		•	•	•		•	•	•	
	Art's public display required																		•		•
	Addresses maintenance/repair	•	•	•				•		•		•			•			•		•	
	Art may be displayed in other buildings	•																			•
	Authorizes administrative agency regulations		•	•				•							•					•	•

14

SUPPORTING POINTS

- Public art beautifies and humanizes public architecture.

- Public artworks are important to the economic vitality of cities, making them more attractive places to live, work, and visit. [2]

- Artworks acquired under percent-for-art acts are highly visible and receive broad public exposure. These programs take art out of museums and into people's everyday lives.

- The citizenry supports public art. In a nationwide survey, 87% agreed that a portion of the construction costs for office buildings should be spent on landscaping, attractive interiors, fountains, artworks, and sculpture. Only 8% disagreed. [3]

- Administrative costs generally are low, and the state receives a tangible asset.

- Percent-for-art programs provide much needed commissions and sales for artists, who are statistically among the most underemployed segments of society.

- A society is remembered by its art. Public art created under state percent-for-art laws is a means of preserving our cultural heritage for future generations.

- State programs set an important example for the private sector to include art in privately funded construction.

- Commissions for state building art projects have greatly furthered artists' careers.

- Percent-for-art has been endorsed by both major political parties in their national platforms.

OTHER CONSIDERATIONS

- Allocating 1% for art may not add a full 1% to the building cost and in some cases may result in no added cost. A mural on a wall may be more expensive than a coat of paint, but that wall does have to be finished or painted. A stained glass window may cost more, but even plain window glass is not inexpensive. A cast cement sculptured wall is usually no more expensive than a flat surfaced wall.

- Quality public art is, almost by its very nature, controversial; historically, public taste and acceptance have lagged behind artistic creativity. Such controversy is not unhealthy. Rather, it is stimulating and educational and ultimately raises the public's cultural awareness.

- Care should be taken to ensure that artists from different regions of the state receive commissions.

"Over a period of time Wisconsin's percent-for-art law will develop artworks to preserve the state's artistic and cultural heritage."

—Wisconsin Representative Carl Otte

1. See Alaska Statutes Sections 35.27.010-35.27.030; California Government Code Sections 15813-15813.7; Colorado Revised Statutes Title 24, Article 80.5, Section 5-101; Connecticut General Statutes Section 4-131a; Florida Statutes Section 255.043; Guam Government Code Sections 320-322; Hawaii Revised Statutes Section 103-8; Illinois Statutes Chapter 127, Section 783.01; Iowa Code Section 304A.10; Maine Revised Statutes Title 27, Chapter 16, Sections 451-459; Massachusetts H. 6575 (1980); Michigan Compiled Laws, Sections 18.71-18.81; Revised Statutes of Nebraska Sections 82-317 to 82-329; New Hampshire Revised Statutes Title 19-A, Sections 8-12; New Jersey Statutes Title 52, Chapter 16A, Sections 29-34; Oregon Revised Statutes Sections 276.073-276.090; South Dakota Statutes Section 5-14-8.1; Texas Codes Title 20, Article 601b, Sections 5.18-5.19; Revised Code of Washington Chapter 43.17, Section 200; Wisconsin Statutes Sections 44.51 and 44.57.

Percent-for-art legislation has been introduced in seventeen other states. In Arizona, Louisiana and Maryland art in public buildings pilot programs have been established without legislation through the state arts agencies.

2. For further discussion of the arts' impact and use as an economic development tool, see page 57.

3. Harris, Louis, Americans and the Arts: A Survey of Public Opinion, American Council for the Arts (1973).

THE ARTS IN EDUCATION

If John Adams thought that the study of the arts would be widely offered in our schools, he would be disappointed that his dream has not yet come true. For although the arts have a demonstrated value in children's development and although the public education system offers perhaps the ideal medium through which the arts can be introduced to children, public school arts education instruction is not universally available in most states.

The Arts Task Force considers expansion of arts education to be among the highest priorities for state legislative action. The Task Force believes that arts experiences foster those qualities most characteristically human — imagination, creativity, and the abilities to conceptualize, reason abstractly, and solve complex problems; that the arts are a pre-eminent means for developing and expressing feelings, intuition, and a sense of beauty; that arts involvement promotes individual discipline and interest in education, and communication and understanding among cultural groups; that the arts have practical value in preparing children to function effectively in our complex, pluralistic, contemporary world; and that the arts therefore belong at the center of our education curriculum.

While most of the education we offer our children concentrates on development of rational and analytic faculties, the arts encourage the growth of perception, intuition, creativity, and the capacity to express feelings. Research has shown the different functions of the two brain hemispheres and points to the arts as a means of developing metaphoric, right-hemisphere thinking balancing the rational, left-hemisphere development emphasized in other school instruction.

The arts have value not only in individual development, but also in improving the entire educational process. Utilizing the arts in an interdisciplinary approach to teach other basic subjects has been highly successful. Examples include teaching reading concepts through animated films and television and through the words of songs and text of plays; using artists to teach the scientific theories of light, color, and sound, principles that are intimate to their art; providing history instruction through ancient art and artifacts that children can reproduce and use as props in dramatic productions illustrating historical events; and learning biology and physiology by drawing parts of the body or by body movement through dance to illustrate the use of muscles.

The arts also deserve a prominent role in special education, for both the gifted and talented and children with learning disabilities. The arts have been effectively used to teach concepts to children unable to learn in the traditional classroom.[1]

The Arts Task Force offers four recommendations for state legislation to improve arts education:

- **Establish arts education as part of basic education within state law;**
- **Fund in-service arts education training for elementary school teachers;**
- **Include artistically gifted and talented children within state gifted and talented programs; and**

● **Consider state funding for schools for the arts.**

The Task Force considers its recommendations to be part of a national movement for arts education and wants to give special recognition to three groups that have fostered this movement: the Arts in Education Program of the John D. Rockefeller 3rd Fund, which was established in 1967; the Alliance for Arts Education, which was created in 1972 under the aegis of the John F. Kennedy Center for the Performing Arts and the U.S. Office of Education (now the federal Department of Education) and which has fostered alliance for arts education committees in most states; and the Arts, Education and Americans Panel, chaired by David Rockefeller, Jr., which in 1977 published *Coming to Our Senses*, considered by many the most important arts education sourcebook to date.

Finally, the Task Force recognizes that arts education will be most effective when it is offered through a comprehensive and sequential approach, beginning at the elementary level and continuing through high school, and when it involves the school and community working in a partnership that includes classroom teachers, arts educators, artists,[2] school administrators, community arts resources, and parents.

"A study by the U.S. Office of Education has shown that the most successful arts education programs are those in which the parents and community members were most actively involved."
— Shirley Trusty Corey, Supervisor Comprehensive Arts in Education Program, Orleans Parish School Board, New Orleans

"Perhaps arts education must begin by the re-education of people to the basic importance of the arts themselves, and this includes the re-education of legislators who are frequently unwilling to admit to the genuine importance of the arts.

Legislation is crucial to the success of arts education, particularly in rough economic times. Priorities must be rearranged to place the arts in education towards the top rather than at the bottom. We must make people aware of the essential role the arts play in an educational system . . . In the development of cognitive, socialization, and self-concept skills. We must, now more than ever before, fight for the place in our educational systems that the arts deserve and need to occupy . . . We, as legislators, must work together with our informed constituents to humanize as well as educate people through the arts . . ."
— Michigan State Senator Jack Faxon

NOTES
1. Arts in special education is more broadly presented in the section "Arts and the Disabled." See pages 92-93.
2. The role of artists in arts education is discussed under the Task Force's Artists-in-Residence Recommendation. See pages 45-46.

ARTS IN BASIC EDUCATION

RECOMMENDATION:
Amend the state education act to redefine basic education to include arts education at the elementary and secondary levels.

The word **basic** is used to identify those subjects essential to our educational system. The Council for Basic Education, a nonprofit organization dedicated to strengthening instruction in basic subjects, endorses the arts as a key element in education and has formally included the arts in its restatement of objectives:

"[T]he arts, properly taught, are basic to individual development since they, more than any other subject, awaken all the senses . . . [T]he arts are basic, right at the heart of the matter."

Despite public opinion in favor of arts instruction[1] and expanding audiences for visual and performing arts events, several misconceptions concerning the arts in education persist among the "reading, writing, arithmetic, and nothing else" proponents.

MYTH: Achievement levels in the traditional basics suffer with the addition or integration of arts instruction.

REALITY: Education programs emphasizing the arts enhance achievement levels. The Arts IMPACT Project, designed by the four national arts education associations and funded by the U.S. Office of Education (now the Department of Education), dramatically demonstrated that the arts improve test scores and achievement levels. After four years of Arts IMPACT, for example, evaluation of an Ohio elementary school showed that the number of sixth graders with a reading vocabulary above grade level rose 65%. In arithmetic computation, the rise was 56%; in arithmetic concepts, 63%; and in reading comprehension, 41%. Arts education projects funded by the John D. Rockefeller 3rd Fund reveal that attitudes, motivation,

and attendance improved among both students and teachers. Programs conducted by the Guggenheim Museum and Community School District in New York City reveal similar findings.

MYTH: The arts lack practical value in education.

REALITY: Study in the arts involves many of the same thought processes used during study in the sciences. These shared processes include observing, describing, comparing, classifying, measuring, inferring, and drawing conclusions. Arts education also provides training for career opportunities, develops communication skills, increases environmental awareness, and builds confidence.

MYTH: Arts education is a frill that ordinary people do not need and that only wealthy people can afford.

REALITY: The arts have intrinsic value as a tool for developing the complete individual. They are universal and human, and promote personal and cultural understanding. By making the arts available to all children, the elitist image of the arts will disappear.

Fifteen states have redefined their education acts to include the arts, and correspondingly, school districts in those states have increased their allocation of funds for arts instruction. Pennsylvania, for instance, spends approximately $140 million on salaries for its 9,500 art, music, theatre, and dance instructors.

North Carolina, although not mandating arts instruction, annually spends more than $80 million for arts supplies, materials, facilities, and salaries for the 2,600 certified arts instructors located in the 2,063 public schools. These monies are supplemented by local funds. An additional $5 million line item will be proposed in the 1981-1982 state budget for elementary school arts specialists.

South Carolina, under its Defined Minimum Program, has appropriated nearly $13 million in state funds for the hiring of art and music, as well as physical education, specialists. The law requires at least one arts specialist for every 800 elementary school students by July, 1982.

Washington State's Basic Education Act of 1977 makes a commitment to arts education without ever using that term.

"The goal of the Basic Education Act for the schools of the state of Washington set forth in this 1977 amendatory act shall be to provide students with the opportunity to achieve those skills which are generally recognized as requisite to learning. Those skills shall include the ability:

● To distinguish, interpret and make use of words, numbers and other symbols, including sound, colors, shapes and textures;

● To organize words and other symbols into acceptable verbal and nonverbal forms of expression, and numbers into their appropriate functions;

● To perform intellectual functions such as problem solving, decision making, goal setting, selecting, planning, predicting, experimenting, ordering and evaluating; and

● To use various muscles necessary for coordinating physical and mental functions."[2]

Some states have adopted position papers endorsed by their superintendent of public instruction and/or state board of education that include the arts as an essential curriculum component. These papers encourage but do not mandate arts instruction by local school districts.

Several states have initiated legislation to generate additional funds. In California, legislation was enacted during 1980 allocating $750,000 annually for three years to develop exemplary arts education programs in local schools.[3] In Michigan, legislation that would have appropriated $350,000 annually for the hiring of arts specialists was twice passed by the legislature but also twice vetoed by the governor.

Other states fund specialized arts instruction. The State of Washington's Cultural Enrichment Program, funded at $1.1 million for the 1979-81 biennium, consists of major cultural companies and repertory ensembles performing in public schools during school hours, an artmobile carrying an art exhibit to schools statewide, and a visiting artists' program employing resident artists in rural schools. The program offers quality arts experiences to elementary and secondary level students and reaches nearly every school district with at least one artform each year.

"In Michigan, the Superintendent of Public Instruction came out with a statement that school districts should be committed to the arts, and then they began to feel that there was more than just one legislator committed to arts education. Both the Legislature and the Superintendent appointed arts education advisory councils to make recommendations."
— Michigan State Senator Jack Faxon

Several states have established arts or cultural divisions within their state educational agencies, reflecting the state's commitment to offering quality arts instruction to all students. The New York State Education Department has organized its Division of the Humanities and the Arts into three bureaus: The Bureau of Art Education, the Bureau of Music Education, and the Humanities and Performing Arts Unit. Each bureau has a unique role in expanding arts education. Some states, including Michigan, New Jersey, Pennsylvania, and Washington, have

New Hampshire's Project AREA and California's Performing Tree are among the many organizations across the country that utilize community resources to bring students live arts experiences by professional artists. South Carolina's SCORE is an example of a state-funded traveling ensemble providing live dramatic performances in schools.

The federal Department of Education has funded collaborative arts projects in approximately ten states. The grants, some to districts that bus students, bring together children with different ethnic backgrounds to work in the classroom on arts projects requiring group participation. In some cases multiracial teams of artists are used as instructors.

"The Cultural Enrichment Program provides funding for arts organizations to visit all of the State's school districts each year. It is an outstanding program, the only one of its kind in the country."
— Washington State Senator Alan Bluechel

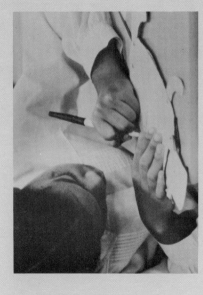

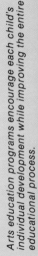

Through the arts, students are permitted to discover a medium in which there is no right or wrong, only individual expression.

Arts education programs encourage each child's individual development while improving the entire educational process.

SUPPORTING POINTS

● The American public overwhelmingly endorses inclusion of the arts in the core curriculum (Harris survey).

● In states that have redefined the education act to include the arts as basic, additional funding for arts education has resulted in school programs that effectively integrate the arts into core curriculum.

● Program evaluation indicates that effective integration of the arts into the school curriculum enhances achievement levels in the traditional basic subjects and improves attitudes, motivation, and attendance of both students and teachers.

● The children of today will be the artists and audiences of tomorrow.

● Inclusion of culture and the arts in basic curriculum represents a more humanistic approach to education.

● Extensive use of community arts resources, including artists and arts institutions and organizations, promotes greater cooperation between the community and school and results in effective arts programs.

NOTES
1. For a discussion of public opinion in favor of arts education, see page 59.
2. *Revised Code of Washington,* Section 28A.58.752.
3. *California Education Code,* Section 8800 and following.

regional educational units that work with both the state and local educational agencies to administer school arts programs. Other states have a cadre of coordinators who work within their respective regions. These structures have proven valuable in promoting and implementing arts education programs.

"The first thing the state department of education needs is professional arts education staff."
— Jack Faxon

"I don't think the public will become supporters of the arts because we tell them the arts are good for the economy or because anyone tells them that the arts are good for their souls or for their social standing. The only way we will effectively develop a broad constituency is through education in the arts . . . We have done the right thing so far in concentrating our energies on the excellence of output in the arts, but unless we now divert some of our energies and funds towards audience development through arts education, we will be unable in 20 years to sustain our wonderful cultural institutions because the necessary public support will be lacking."
— David Rockefeller, Jr.

RECOMMENDATION:

Make state funds available to interested school districts to provide in-service arts education training for elementary school teachers.

Training programs should emphasize both arts experiences and appreciation, and integration of the arts into the educational curriculum as a means of teaching math, reading, science, and other basic subjects.

Many elementary school teachers have no participatory experience in the arts and no teacher training in arts education — *Coming to Our Senses* estimates that 30 percent of new teachers are not required to take a single art or music class prior to teacher certification. Elliot Eisner, a nationally recognized authority on arts education, states the problem succinctly:

"When one realizes that many elementary teachers had their last exposure to a trained art teacher at the junior high school level, that the majority of them studied no art at the secondary level, that a substantial proportion have had no training in art education at the university level, and that supervision and consultation in art education at the school district level is being drastically curtailed, the magnitude of the problem begins to emerge."[1]

Moreover, these teachers, because they are unprepared, are understandably afraid to teach or use the arts in their classrooms and consequently spend little if any time on the arts.

"Many teachers do not know how to plan an arts curriculum because they were never taught how to do so . . . They think art is something you do on Friday afternoon when the kids are antsy. They don't realize that there is a natural sequence to teaching the arts just like there is for math or reading."
— Beverly Schoonover, Associate Professor of Arts Education, University of New Mexico

Furthermore, downward trends in student enrollment and teacher turnover indicate a more stable teacher population in the 1980's. Given these factors, in-service teacher training must play a major role in preparing current classroom teachers to offer meaningful arts education.

In 1980, legislation was introduced in New Mexico to provide $160,000 in state funds to interested school districts for in-service arts education teacher training. The bill, SB 9, passed the Senate but was held by a House committee because of an unrelated controversy; it will be reintroduced during 1981. SB 9 would have implemented an in-service teacher training model developed by the Lincoln Center Institute in New York City.[2]

"Since I first was elected to the Legislature and served on the Education Committee, I have been bothered about the lack of arts education in our public schools. For some reason it has almost disappeared. I think it happened without us knowing. I searched and searched for a system through which the Legislature could try to introduce arts education back into the public schools. At the Task Force's New York meeting, I finally found what I thought was the answer to this problem when we visited the Lincoln Center and learned from Mr. Mark Schubart about the Lincoln Center Institute . . .

I saw a chance to perhaps use the same system in New Mexico. I went home and called a group of people together that I knew to be interested in the same subject . . . and we worked out a plan . . .

We decided to start at the elementary level with 100 elementary teachers, and the next year go to 200 teachers . . . We hoped in a few years to have hundreds of teachers in the New Mexico system who had been through the program.

We prepared a bill . . . (that) sailed through the Education and Finance Committees and the floor of the Senate. I don't think I had

"We need a conceptual base for integration of the arts into the curriculum . . . How does music relate to physics and mathematics relate to form, line, color, space, balance, rhythm, and harmony? There needs to be a lot of work at the conceptual level with curriculum developers to show teachers how all these subjects relate."

— Anne Taylor, Professor of Arts Education, University of New Mexico

Teachers attending an in-service arts education workshop learn how to relate the arts to school children.

NOTES

1. Eisner, Elliot W. "The State of Art Education Today and Some Potential Remedies," 31 *Art Education* 14, at 15 (December 1978)

2. The Lincoln Center Institute's in-service process brings teachers from interested schools and school districts together in all-day, three-week summer sessions at Lincoln Center. Workshops in the various disciplines are conducted by professional artists. The teachers view each of a series of performances twice and participate in seminars about each work and about the philosophy of arts education and its relationship to the total school curriculum. In the seminars, the teachers perform in multiple disciplines, gaining a first-hand understanding of the artist creating. The teachers, continuing in partnership with the Institute's faculty and staff, then develop detailed curricular plans for work with their own students during the ensuing school year. To help the teachers revise and continue to develop their own arts education curricula, they are encouraged to re-enroll for subsequent summer workshops. The Institute, using government and private funding, shares the program costs with participating school districts.

3. For examples of using the arts as an interdisciplinary approach, see page 17.

SUPPORTING POINTS

● In-service training is an accepted, documented means of teacher preparation. State funding of in-service programs is common.

● While many state teacher licensing provisions do establish minimum teacher-training subject-matter requirements, most do not include training in the arts among the requirements. In-service training in the arts will fill this void in many educators' pre-certification training.

● In-service arts education training expands teachers' understanding of themselves and their ability to communicate with their students.

● With in-service arts education training, many teachers will experience a renewed vitality and motivation in approaching their profession.

● In-service training is an important and effective means for utilizing existing personnel in developing comprehensive arts education programs.

● When accomplished on a district-wide basis, in-service arts education training promotes communication and cooperation among teachers and administrators and interaction between the school and community.

● Arts education teacher training introduces an interdisciplinary approach to teaching and learning that is both effective and stimulating.[3]

one vote in the Senate against the bill. We got it . . . to the House Appropriations Committee at the same time that the committee had cut the state arts division's budget to a dollar because of a controversial art exhibit in Albuquerque . . . So they killed the bill, but we are going to get it through next year . . . The chairman of the interim committee on education told me that they will carry the bill as a committee bill."

— New Mexico Senator John Irick

Successful in-service programs share certain features.

● The programs are directed toward interested school districts.

● Their main emphasis is on developing teachers' ability to relate the arts to school children by instilling a sense of what it means to create as an artist does.

● The programs have begun with at least partial outside funding, which has gradually been assumed by the local school districts.

● They involve or at least encourage follow-up sessions or continual arts education training.

● The programs stimulate classroom interaction between elementary teachers and professional artists.

PROGRAMS FOR CHILDREN
GIFTED AND TALENTED IN THE ARTS

RECOMMENDATION:
Include children gifted and talented in the arts within categorical state funding of gifted and talented programs.

According to the Arts Task Force Survey of *State Arts Programs, Legislation, and Activities,* 15 states mandate special instruction for the artistically gifted and talented.[1] These states generally provide funding for accelerated classes, enrichment courses, independent studies, or mentorships conducted at the district level. Other states have established schools for the arts as the central part of their gifted and talented program.[2]

SUPPORTING POINTS

- Visual and performing arts is one of the six categories of giftedness designated by the United States Commissioner of Education in the 1971 report to Congress that preceded the establishment of state gifted and talented programs.

- The artistically gifted and talented children of today are the artists, musicians, actors, dancers, writers, poets and craftspeople of tomorrow.

- Many artistically gifted students are not challenged by a traditional curriculum and will drop out before completing their secondary education unless they are provided special programs. Classroom teachers, too, are frustrated in trying to provide a stimulating curriculum for these students.

- In the past, many artists have been forced to pursue other vocations in order to finance their training. Some aspiring artists have been permanently channeled into these secondary vocations.

- By offering programs to the artistically gifted and talented through our public schools, we provide these children an alternative to private arts instruction. Gifted programs may be the only way economically disadvantaged students have of developing their artistic talents.

- Gifted and talented programs in the arts are consistent with the evolution of the American public educational system toward the goal of addressing the special needs of each child.

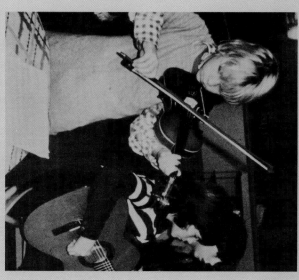

Through gifted and talented programs, the artistically gifted children of today have the opportunity to develop the talents necessary to become the artists and performers of tomorrow.

NOTES:
1. The chart on pages 10-11 indicates the 15 states. Among the statutory provisions referring to the artistically gifted are *California Education Code* Section 52202; *Iowa Code* Sections 442.31 to 442.33; *Code of Maryland,* Article 8, Section 201; *Oregon Revised Statutes* Sections 343.391 to 343.399.
2. *Schools for the Arts,* another Task Force recommendation, is presented next.

SCHOOLS FOR THE ARTS

RECOMMENDATION:

Consider funding schools for the arts to provide intensive training opportunities for artistically gifted and talented school-age children. The schools may be organized as (1) summer schools for the arts, (2) schools where a substantial portion of the day is devoted to arts instruction, or (3) after-school arts instruction programs.

In 1965 the North Carolina School of the Arts became the first state created and funded arts school in the nation.[1] Since then, at least two other states, Alabama and Florida, have established state arts schools, and another, New Jersey, has enacted legislation authorizing such a school. Other states, including New York,[2] Oklahoma, Pennsylvania, and South Carolina, operate summer schools for the arts, and local

school districts in some states administer public arts schools that receive state funding. Some state arts schools also derive a portion of their funding from private sources.

Most of the state schools and programs offer talented young people, who are seriously considering a professional arts career, instruction in a wide range of performing, visual, and literary artforms.

SUPPORTING POINTS

- State-funded schools for the arts allow artistically gifted students to receive intensive instruction in order to develop their specialized abilities and realize their full potential. The intensive training instills in the young people the discipline and dedication necessary to pursue a career in the arts.

- Schools for the arts offer talented children an opportunity to work with and learn from master artists and teachers as well as their gifted peers. The schools attract high-caliber artists as teachers, and the master-apprentice relationships ensure continuity and progression of our cultural heritage.

- Arts schools teach students that arts and academics are both important in creating a well-rounded individual. The arts, whenever possible, are integrated into the study of traditional academic areas, creating a renewed interest in subjects many exceptional children find boring.

- State arts schools are often the professional training ground for artists of the major performing arts companies and guarantee our arts institutions a continuous stream of quality performers.

- Students who cannot afford tuition and living expenses may attend state-supported schools on scholarships that provide training opportunities not otherwise available.

- Students who attend state arts schools act as cultural ambassadors and are highly effective in helping to infuse the arts into their schools and communities.

- State arts schools promote a partnership between state education and arts agencies, often receiving funding from both.

"I was responsible for the law creating the Summer School for the Arts Program in my state. Originally it was at the high school level only. Our most talented youngsters in the high schools were selected through statewide competition to go to Saratoga for the summer to receive instruction from the top individual artists of the Philadelphia Orchestra, New York City Ballet, and the other companies. The program now includes the university and college level. At an annual cost of about $1.6 million we are giving an opportunity to better than 500 youngsters in New York to really develop the skills that they have. It's a magnificent program."

— New York Assemblyman William Passannante

NOTES

1. *North Carolina General Statutes Sections 116-63 and 116-64.*

2. *New York Education Code Sections 4450-4451.*

ARTISTS' RIGHTS

"Artists Rights Today" by Robert Rauschenberg.

"Why should a visual artist receive special attention? Because, almost by definition, being an artist precludes practical calculation or pecuniary gain. An artist must pursue the urgings of his muse or attempt to have it exorcised. It is incongruous that artworks are protected, insured, bonded, crated, and guarded — such care is taken with the inanimate art object — while the human artist is treated as dispensable. So much money is spent on eulogies and death anniversary celebrations, but what is being done to help the artist stay alive and productive?"

— *Rubin Gorewitz, Founder and President, Artists Rights Today, Inc.*

To protect artists' rights, the Arts Task Force has adopted four recommendations for state legislation.

RECOMMENDATION:

Provide protection to artists who give their works to art dealers on consignment to sell or exhibit. The dealer acts as a trustee in holding the art and funds from sales. Some laws also protect artists against loss or damage to the artworks while in the dealers' possession and against claims by dealers' creditors.

Eight states have enacted laws defining the relationship between an artist and art dealer when the artist provides artworks for a dealer to sell or exhibit. Six statutes specify that a consignment relationship is created with the dealer acting as an agent and trustee in holding the artist's works and funds from their sale.

The main purpose of these laws is to assist artists in collecting money to which they are entitled. A dealer who misappropriates an artist's funds becomes subject, as an agent and trustee, to civil damages and criminal prosecution for embezzlement.

With respect to consigned art, the laws also generally prohibit the dealer's creditors from claiming the art or proceeds from its sale, hold the dealer in possession responsible for its loss or damage, require the artist and dealer to agree on a payment

ARTIST-ART DEALER RELATIONS LAWS (through 1980)

PROVISIONS	California (Civil Code Sec. 1738-1738.9)	Connecticut (Sec. 42-116k-116m)	Massachusetts (Mass. Ann. Laws, Ch 104A)	Michigan (Sec. 19.410(1)-19.410(5))	New Mexico (NM Stat., Ch. 56, Art. 11, Sec. 1-3)	New York (NY Gen. Bus. Law, Sec. 219-219a)	Texas (Title 132, Art. 9018)	Wisconsin (Wisc. Stat. Ch. 129)
The transfer of an artwork to a dealer for sale or exhibition to the public constitutes a consignment.	●	●	●	●		●		●
The art dealer is the artist's agent in holding the work for sale.	●	●	●	●		●		●
The art dealer acts as a trustee in holding money from the sale of consigned art until the artist is paid in full.	●	●	●	●		●		●
The art dealer is responsible for loss or damage while holding consigned art.	●	●	●			●		●
Consigned art and the proceeds from its sale are exempt from the claims of the art dealer's creditors.	●	●	●		●	●	●	●
The artist receives his or her share of the proceeds first in an installment sale, unless otherwise agreed in writing.	●	●	●					●
A waiver of rights by the artist is void.	●	●	●	●[1]		●[1]		●
A written contract between the artist and dealer is required and must specify (1) a minimum sale price, (2) a payment schedule, (3) the dealer's responsibility for loss or damage while holding the art, and (4) the need for the artist's consent before use or display of consigned art.	●		●	●	●	●	●	●
Provides a broad definition of art which includes crafts and mixed media works.	●	●	●	●	●	●	●	●
The artist's rights pass to heirs after death.	●	●	●	●	●	●	●	●
Excludes auction sales.	●	●				●		●
Specifies a $50 minimum penalty for violation plus actual damages and attorneys' fees.	●		●					●
Applies to contracts entered into after the law's effective date and may apply to prior contracts.	●		●	●		●		●

1. A limited waiver is permitted.

schedule, and void any waiver of rights by the artist.

While providing protection to artists, the laws have not adversely affected reputable art dealers. They do, however, make it more difficult for disreputable dealers to take advantage of artists with impunity.

The chart on the preceding page contrasts provisions of the existing laws.

"Any working artist can tell you that the biggest point of difficulty with the dealer is getting dealers to account accurately and faithfully for work consigned by the artist, and for proceeds from sale of the artist's work... This is a constant problem and preoccupation of working artists.
—Stanford University Law Professor John Merryman*

"This law makes clear that if there is a theft or if there's damage to the work of art on consignment, the risk of loss is to be borne by the dealer. This is important because artists are frequently unable or can't afford to procure insurance for works on consignment. The dealer can procure insurance; it may be expensive, it may be the dealer chooses to self-insure, but the risk of loss is clearly placed upon the dealer."
—Golden Gate University Law Professor Thomas Goetzl

SUPPORTING POINTS

● Art dealers experiencing financial difficulties may not inform artists of the sale of their works. The trust and agency relationships created by these laws increase the likelihood of notice and payment to artists.

● Without the benefit of this law, artists are reluctant, for professional and economic reasons, to take legal action against dealers. The law provides artists with a means to press for money due, even absent a written agreement.

● Without this statute, artists not infrequently lose consigned art or proceeds from its sale to dealers' bankruptcy creditors, unless artists comply with the filing requirements of Uniform Commercial Code Section 2-326. While this result may be justified in commercial transactions between individuals generally engaged in business, it is not appropriate between parties with greatly differing business skills.

● Between the artist and dealer, the latter is in a better position to insure consigned art against loss or damage. Holding dealers liable regardless of fault prevents their contractually disclaiming responsibility for loss or damage caused by their negligence.

"One of the big abuses is that the art dealer will operate on the capital that is engendered from sales of consigned art. In other words they will sell the work and it will be 60, 80, 90 days, six months sometimes, before the artist gets his money. Through this particular bill, the first money received by the dealer usually must go to the artist; the dealer gets his share when full collection is made. It's a very important law from our point of view."
— Ron Blumberg, Founder and Past President, Artists for Economic Action

"Under the commercial codes of each state, an artist, in order to be protected in a bankruptcy situation, has to fill out a form for each piece of his or her work on consignment in every gallery. Now, as a printmaker I may have 100 pieces of art going in and out of galleries all the time, and I have to be concerned about filling all these pieces of paper to put possible creditors on notice. There are cases where galleries have gone under, and because these forms are not filled out, and it's just not done by artists, the consigned works have gone to the creditors."
—Shirley Levy, Boston Visual Artists Association

ARTISTS' LIVE-WORK SPACE

RECOMMENDATION:

Allow local governments to establish zones where artists may live and work in buildings in urban areas previously zoned for commercial and/or industrial use and to authorize alternative building code requirements in those areas.

"Artists are being taken advantage of. They move into a depressed area, fix it up with studios, the area becomes attractive — coffee houses, galleries, boutiques move in — and we get moved out because we can't afford increasingly higher rent demands. In fact, we're the first stage of urban renewal and we get kicked out for our pains."
— An artist attending a San Francisco live-work conference.

"SoHo was a run down area where artists moved in sub rosa in violation of existing zoning and housing laws and were living in commercial buildings. I am sure there is plenty of property like this in every other old city in America, loft-type buildings that are unused today with large amounts of vacant space. With enabling legislation from the state legislature and cooperation from the city planning department or commission, there can be a change in the zoning providing for mixed residential and commercial use."
— New York Assemblyman William Passannante

Fifth Century B.C. excavations in Athens have revealed houses containing artists' and artisans' workshops and entire districts devoted to specific crafts. During the 1960's in the SoHo district in Lower Manhattan, large manufacturing lofts, many of which were being abandoned by businesses leaving the city, became a prime location for artists seeking inexpensive studio space. From SoHo, this phenomenon has spread to other urban areas throughout the country.

Visual and performing artists have special locational needs. They require large areas of work and storage space for the practice of their art. Yet their income is frequently limited and cannot support both a residence and a studio. Their needs are well served by joint living and working quarters, particularly if a large amount of space is available at low rents. This was the case in SoHo in the 1960's and is true in many central city areas in the 1980's.

The public also benefits from the artists' influx into run-down commercial areas. Conversion of space to joint living and working quarters provides a new use for decaying structures and encourages building rehabilitation. The relocation of visual and performing artists into downtown areas leads to a resurgence of cultural activities in those areas, aiding in the central city's revitalization.[1]

Recognizing the needs of artists and potential public benefits, New York and California[2] have enacted enabling laws permitting local governments to rezone commercial and industrial areas for use as both working and residential space and to adopt alternative building, health, and safety regulations consistent with their

residential use. The New York law, enacted in 1964 and since amended four times, is more specific and restrictive in specifying building, health, and safety requirements. In contrast the 1979 California statute requires only minimum kitchen and bathroom facilities but permits local government to specify other standards.

Some considerations that should be addressed by state legislatures considering live-work measures are:

● Should occupancy of live-work space be limited to artists? How is an artists-only limitation to be defined and enforced? New York has tried an artist certification procedure without success.

● How can artists who lease and rehabilitate decaying buildings for live-work use avoid becoming the victims of their own revitalization efforts? Renovation and conversion to residential use often increases property values. When rents in turn escalate, artists are forced to relocate.

This cycle has occurred in New York City, and the problem has become so severe that in 1980, the state legislature passed a measure imposing in live-work areas a one-year moratorium on rent increases and protection against tenants' eviction. The moratorium's purpose is to allow local authorities time to determine a long-term solution. Possible solutions include more permanent rent controls (historically unsuccessful), using government loan subsidies and other incentives to encourage purchase of live-work buildings by artists and artists' cooperatives, and long-term leases.

- Should property tax abatement provisions and other state tax incentives, such as accelerated depreciation for income tax purposes, be adopted to encourage building owners and artists to rehabilitate commercial and industrial buildings? New York's law offers owners a twelve-year exemption from increased property tax assessments resulting from building improvements.

- Is a live-work zone for artists a permissible state zoning classification or is it discriminatory legislation violative of equal protection standards? (A statement of legislative intent such as that found in the New York and California statutes will likely withstand constitutional challenge.)

- Should live-work occupancies be limited to specific zones, or should they be permitted citywide?

- Should live-work statutes also provide for conversion of residential housing to studio use?

- Zoning revision is not enough. A flexible approach toward health, safety, and occupancy standards is required if conversion of vacant commercial and industrial space to residential living is to be economically feasible. How can building code standards be relaxed consistent with government's responsibility to protect the public health and safety and artists' financial ability to provide rehabilitation?

"Most artists simply cannot afford the cost of code compliance."
—Arielda Sikora, City Planner for Los Angeles

SUPPORTING POINTS

- Artists' live-work enclaves can help revitalize portions of decaying inner cities and other depressed areas, providing an active cultural environment.

- Artists' conversion, rehabilitation, and use of existing structures are preferable to demolition and new construction, the inevitable result of continued decay and neglect of older buildings.

- Allowing artists to renovate vacant, decaying buildings is a cost-efficient urban renewal method that can have a profound, beneficial economic impact on central city areas.

- Artists' live-work statutes, if carefully drawn, can effectively advance historic preservation principles.

- Forcing artists to live under illegal conditions encourages disrespect for the law and creates the constant threat of discovery and ultimate eviction. Government should attempt to legitimate this significant, positive phenomenon.

- With present and projected energy costs and limitations, the live-work movement, among artists and others, will likely become more widespread. The 1970 census found 2% of the population working out of residences. This number includes doctors, lawyers, inventors, caterers, mechanics, mail order and telephone answering services, disabled persons, and parents working while caring for children.

NOTES

1. For a discussion of the arts' economic development role, see pages 57-58.

2. *New York Multiple Dwelling Law,* Article 7-B, Sections 275-279; *California Health and Safety Code* Section 17958.11. Article 22 of the *Massachusetts State Building Code* acknowledges that buildings erected before codes were enacted cannot comply strictly with the standards applicable to new residential buildings. This recognition has facilitated residential use of older commercial buildings, although artists must still apply for live-work occupancy through local agencies. Minneapolis and Seattle have adopted ordinances permitting artists' residential use of commercial and industrial buildings.

ART PRESERVATION

RECOMMENDATION: Provide artists, and in some cases the public, the right to bring legal action against intentional physical defacement, alteration, or destruction by government or private owners of artworks of recognized quality. Both injunctive relief and action for damages may be authorized. Sometimes referred to as "Artists' Moral Rights."

In 1958 a private collector donated the Alexander Calder mobile "Pittsburgh" for placement in the Pittsburgh, Pennsylvania airport. The Airport Commission positioned the mobile differently from the way Calder had intended, immobilized it, and repainted the black and white artwork in green and gold, Pittsburgh's official colors. Although Calder was furious about the changes, he had no legal recourse against the Commission.

In April 1980, the Isamu Noguchi aluminum sculpture "Shinto," which had been suspended in the lobby of the Bank of Tokyo's New York City branch, was cut down, chopped into several pieces, and relegated to a warehouse, all without the artist's prior knowledge or consent. Noguchi's comment upon learning of the action: "It's vandalism, and very reactionary. I should think they'd ask the artist before they did something like that." A representative of the bank reportedly said that Noguchi had not been told of the decision because "the sculpture is the property of the bank." Noguchi agreed that he too had no legal recourse.

Under the laws of more than 60 European and Latin American countries, and also of California, both Calder and Noguchi would have a legal remedy.

The California Art Preservation Act,[1] effective January 1, 1980, allows artists to bring legal action against government and private owners to prevent their works from being intentionally injured or destroyed and to collect money damages when the art has already been harmed. The statute also:

- Applies only to original paintings, sculpture, and drawings of recognized quality;
- Provides rights during the artist's lifetime and, for 50 years after his or her death, to the artist's estate;
- Excludes commercial art created under a work-for-hire arrangement;
- Requires a written and recorded agreement between the artist and owner for protection of murals and other art that cannot easily be removed from buildings;

"There were technical objections that had to be worked out, such as museum conservation of art and art attached to buildings."
— Golden Gate University Law Professor Thomas Goetzl, who drafted the California Art Preservation Act.

- Enables professionals to frame, conserve, and restore art without liability unless they are grossly negligent;
- Allows artists to waive their rights in writing;
- Permits artists to alter or destroy their works prior to sale; and
- Authorizes a court to award attorneys' and expert witness fees.

The law also gives the artist the right to claim or disclaim authorship — the so-called right of paternity. This right was exercised, for example, by sculptor David Smith in 1960 after he learned that, subsequent to its sale, his sculpture "17h's" had been stripped of its original cadmium red color. Smith angrily renounced creation

of the sculpture, branded it a ruin, and called for laws to protect artists against such intentional acts.

A unique feature of the California act awards compensatory damages arising from a lawsuit to the artist, but allocates any punitive damages to nonprofit arts-related institutions selected by the court.

"To pass this law, you have to get legislators to rethink their concepts of property rights. Property rights are very strong in this country, and that's why we have not adopted art preservation laws. You have to begin to think that maybe the person who created the work of art, and perhaps also the public, retain some interest in seeing that the art is not destroyed, not mutilated, and not changed without the artist's consent. The first impression that members of the judiciary committee had when we presented our bill was 'It's mine, I can do anything with it, I can cut it up if it's too big for a certain place that I want to put it.' But gradually the committee members recognized what we were trying to say and accepted it."

— California State Senator Alan Sieroty

SUPPORTING POINTS

● An artistic creation is more than a tangible, economic commodity; it is a unique expression of the artist's personality. To alter or destroy an artwork intentionally is offensive to the artist and equivalent to a libel against his or her reputation.

● Alteration of art deprives the public of its right to see the work as the artist intended.

● Art preservation statutes are a natural complement to historic preservation laws.

● Artists' lack of bargaining power necessitates art preservation statutes. Even if an artist gains this protection through contract, it is often difficult to assert the reserved rights against subsequent purchasers unless statutory safeguards exist.

OTHER IMPORTANT CONSIDERATIONS

● Should the public be given a legal right to protect important works of art, especially when the artist is not alive or, as in the case of Los Angeles' Watts Towers, not interested? If so, who should enforce the public right: private citizens, government agencies, or both? Should it be limited to artworks in public view? Should it exist in perpetuity as a recognition that the public's interest in important art usually increases as time passes?[2]

● Foreign art preservation laws establish the artist's right as inalienable; the California law allows the artist to waive those rights. Will experienced purchasers routinely require artists to sign waivers?

● Which artforms should be protected? Should art preservation laws also apply to photographs, graphics, crafts, and works in mixed media?

● State art preservation laws are probably not preempted by the Federal Copyright Act since the rights granted are not "equivalent" to those contained in the federal law.[3]

NOTES

1. *California Civil Code Section 987.* Several states impose criminal penalties for defacing art on public or private property or displayed in a public place. A representative statute is *Oklahoma Statutes,* Title 21, Sections 1784 and 1785.

2. Some foreign art preservation laws provide for a government inventory of important artworks. Selected works are protected through a registry system that is similar to the registers of historically significant buildings that have been created by the federal and some state and local governments. The foreign inventories include both publicly and privately owned works, regardless of whether they are in public view. As an incentive for private owners to cooperate, governments agree to provide insurance for and maintenance and restoration of protected art.

3. See the 1976 copyright revisions, *United States Code Annotated,* Title 17, Section 301 (a).

RECOMMENDATION:

Provide artists with a percentage of the resale price of their artworks, provided that the resale is profitable to the seller and the resale price is in excess of a specific minimum amount.

"What would have happened if Robert Rauschenberg had stopped painting in 1958? What are the chances that 'Thaw' would have resold 16 years later for $85,000? It is Rauschenberg's history as an artist, his investment in his career, that gave reason for the market value of 'Thaw' to rise. In this respect artists earn a royalty on the resale."

—Richard Mayer, West Coast Regional Vice-President, Artists Equity Association

"In my lifetime as a working visual artist, there are a very limited number of works that I can create. It is not like designing a refrigerator and allowing mass production to happen . . . Artists should not be denied part of the increasing value from these few pieces of art that we have created."

— Shirley Levy, Boston Visual Artists Union

In 1958 Robert Scull, New York businessman and art collector, purchased Robert Rauschenberg's painting, "Thaw," for $900. In 1973 Scull sold it for $85,000. Rauschenberg got nothing on the resale. Another example is the resale of a Jasper Johns' painting. In September 1980 "Three Flags" was purchased for $1 million, an amount believed to be the highest price paid for a living artist's work. The Connecticut couple who sold the painting to the Whitney Museum of American Art had purchased it in 1959 for $915! Johns, too, does not profit from the resale.

Resale royalties is the most controversial of the recommended legislation affecting artists' rights. Introduced in ten states and in Congress, but thus far enacted only by California,[1] such royalty legislation allocates living artists a percentage of their works' resale price (5% in California) if (1) the resale is profitable to the seller and (2) the resale price exceeds a specific amount.

Resale royalty statutes have existed in Europe since the 1920's and are currently in effect in France, Germany, Italy, and eight other nations. This *droit de suite*, which roughly translates as "proceeds' right," is equivalent in concept to the residual financial interest retained by a composer, an author of a book or play, or other artists when their works are performed, broadcast, or reproduced.

In California the law, which is supported by most artists but opposed by most dealers, applies only to original paintings, sculpture, or drawings resold either in California or by a seller who resides in California. In a lawsuit filed shortly after its January 1, 1977 effective date, a cadre of collectors and dealers challenged the law's constitutionality on several grounds, including preemption by the Federal Copyright Act. However, both a Los Angeles federal district court and the Ninth Circuit Court of Appeals have upheld the act's constitutionality.[2] In October, 1980, the United States Supreme Court refused to grant a hearing.

California's statute also (1) prevents the artist from waiving the royalty, unless an amount greater than 5% is provided for by written contract; (2) requires the California Arts Council to help in locating artists entitled to royalties if sellers are unable to do so; (3) allows an artist to sue to collect a royalty within the later of three years after the resale or one year after its discovery; and (4) applies to artworks created both before and after its operative date.

Not only does the California law not significantly impair any federal interest, but it is the very type of innovative lawmaking that our federalist system is designed to encourage. The California Legislature evidently felt that a need existed to offer further encouragement to, and economic protection of, artists. That is a decision which the courts shall not lightly reverse. An important index of the moral and cultural strength of a people is their official attitude toward, and nurturing of, a free and vital community of artists. The California Resale Royalties Act may be a small positive step in such a direction.

— Federal District Court Judge Robert Tagasuki

Morseburg v. Balyon, March 23, 1978

"The objections that are being raised to resale royalties today are precisely the objections raised in 1909 when it was proposed to compel radio stations that were just beginning to pay royalties upon the performance of music. There was a great furor that, if royalties have to be paid, nobody is going to play music. That's not turned out to be the case. The radio stations play music, and one of the two performing rights collection agencies — ASCAP or BMI — collect royalties that are distributed on a proportionate basis to the artists who are responsible for the creations. So the objections have all been heard before, and time has tested them, and they have not proved meritorious."

— Golden Gate University Law Professor Thomas Goetzl

"It is said that resale royalties would not help poor artists. Well, true. It is said that resale royalties are un-American. On the contrary, it's almost un-American to oppose this issue. We live in a capitalist time when the rich do get richer. . . . The benefit for artists is that, as Robert Rauschenberg said, 'I wasn't always Robert Rauschenberg.' The artist does not know at the outset who will be rich and in a position to get richer."

— Thomas Goetzl

NOTES

1. California Civil Code Section 986. The California law provides artists 5% of the gross sales price on profitable resales over $1,000. Another method, which may be more equitable but also more difficult to enforce, would be to allocate to the artist a percentage of the seller's gross or net profit.

2. Morseburg v. Balyon, U.S. Ninth Circuit Court of Appeals, 621 F.2d 972 (1980).

SUPPORTING POINTS

Because the public is generally slow to understand and appreciate art, artists often are unable initially to sell their works at a fair price. The resale royalty in part remedies this situation and allows artists to benefit as their work appreciates.

Artists have an inherent disadvantage in bargaining and are often in too weak a position to extract resale royalties by contract.

Resale royalties grant legal recognition to the continuing relationship between artists and their works.

The state has an interest in encouraging artistic endeavor, and the resale royalty, by rewarding artists who produce, furthers this interest.

In time the resale royalty will be accepted. Current sentiment against resale royalties is not unlike the initial reaction against the 1909 Copyright Act. Today, copyright is universally accepted in the arts and literature. Proceeds to artists from resale royalties are not great, but they do have symbolic value. Asserting this economic right through the law forces a reassessment of the artist's proper role within the marketplace. This utility far exceeds the economic benefit it confers.

Contrary to critics' predictions, no evidence exists that the California Resale Royalties Act has harmed the California art market.

OTHER CONSIDERATIONS

While the California law is dependent on resale during the artist's lifetime, resale royalty rights perhaps should accrue to heirs following the artist's death. An appropriate period might be fifty years, as now applies to copyright under the 1976 federal revisions.

The most difficult issue is enforcement. The artist may not become aware of a resale and even if the artist does and the seller does not voluntarily pay, the money involved may not justify the expense of a lawsuit, unless state law includes reasonable attorney's fees as part of the award. If a significant number of states or the federal government enact resale royalty laws, a likely result might be the formation of art royalty collection companies similar to ASCAP and BMI.

"It's not a poorer artists' bill, but the young artists and poor artists still applaud it, because it gives them some hope, some faith that perhaps one day they will be able to benefit from it. They think it's important to them. I think the major point is that we are recognizing the creators, we are giving respect to creativity, we are continuing the connection that artists feel towards their work and giving recognition to that in a financial way . . . It seems to me unjust that the creator does not share in the economic system that allows these tremendous profits to be made on his or her work. Five percent is not a very large amount."

— California Senator Alan Sieroty, author of the California Resale Royalties Act

TAX LEGISLATION

The 1970's saw artists expressing great concern about perceived inequities in tax laws affecting artists and their families. The discrimination was exemplified by income tax laws that restricted deductions for charitable donations of artists' works to the cost of materials used in producing the art, while, at the same time, death taxes were levied against the same art at what artists considered an inflated fair market value.

The Arts Task Force offers two recommendations regarding artists' taxes.

RECOMMENDATION:
Enable professional artists, for state income tax purposes, to deduct the fair market value of artworks they create and donate to museums and other charitable organizations. Current law limits the artists' tax deduction to the cost of materials.

In 1979 and 1980, five states — Kansas, Oregon, California, Maryland, and Michigan[1] — changed their laws to allow artists a full fair market value charitable contribution deduction for donated art. Other states are expected to follow suit during the next several years.

Until 1969 the income tax laws allowed artists the greater deduction. However, that year the federal law was changed, and within several years, most states applied the cost-of-materials rule. South Carolina, through regulations, retained the fair market value deduction.

In contrast, in 1969, Ireland exempted resident creative artists from payment of all income taxes attributable to the sale of their artwork. The exemption applies to musical compositions, choreographies, authors' new works, paintings, sculpture, and other visual art. Artists pay a tax on income earned from non-art sources. The law does not affect singers, dancers, actors, and other performing artists.

Artists are frequently asked to donate artworks but feel penalized in being unable to take the same deduction provided to art collectors. Not surprisingly, after 1969, donations by artists to museums and other public institutions have dropped dramatically. For example, New York's Museum of Modern Art experienced a decline of over 90% in the number of creator-donated works.

Qualifications for the deduction differ under the five state laws and South Carolina's regulations. The five statutes require an independent appraisal to substantiate the value of the donated art. Kansas limits

"It's very hard to imagine why a well-to-do collector can take a fair market value deduction, and an artist cannot."
— Henry Hopkins, Director, San Francisco Museum of Modern Art

"Nothing would help America's art museums more than the artist having that right (to take a fair market value deduction)."
— Henry Hopkins

NOTES
1. See *Kansas Statutes*, Chapter 79-32.120; *Oregon Revised Statutes*, Chapter 316.064; *California Revenue and Taxation Code* Section 17216.2; *Code of Maryland* Article 81, Section 281; and *Michigan Compiled Laws*, Section 206.260. As of 1980, Alaska, Connecticut, Florida, Nevada, New Hampshire, South Dakota, Tennessee, Texas, Wyoming, and Washington did not have a state income tax.

qualifying donations to nonprofit galleries and museums supported by public funds, and Maryland, to museums in the state open to the general public. The other four states allow donations to museums, other charities, and government agencies.

California and Maryland limit the fair market value deduction to artists who earn a significant portion of income from the sale of their art, and Maryland further limits the deduction for donated artworks to 50% of the artist's gross income that year. South Carolina, California, and Maryland qualify artistic, literary, and musical creations for the increased artist tax deduction, while Kansas and Oregon limit the higher deduction to visual art.

Michigan's law actually allows a tax credit rather than a deduction under that state's unusual income tax law. The credit is for 50% of the art's fair market value and is limited to the lesser of 20% of the taxpayer's state income tax liability or $100 ($200 for a married couple filing jointly).

SUPPORTING POINTS

- A fair market value state income tax deduction for donated artworks offers artists a measure of tax fairness by providing them the same income tax treatment as collectors receive.

- The valuation of art for gift and death tax purposes is fair market value, and, in order to achieve consistency, this same valuation should be used for charitable contributions.

- The resulting state revenue loss is insignificant. In California, for example, annual state revenue loss was estimated at $10,000-$40,000 out of a more than $20 billion state budget.

- Increasing the allowable deduction will encourage artists' donations to museums, other public institutions, and government, so that the public may enjoy the art.

- Tax laws are used to meet society's economic and social needs and consequently favor certain taxpayers. Encouraging artists to share their work with the public serves an important social goal.

- Changing state income tax law may spur Congress to restore the prior federal law.

- Artists' works are capable of objective valuation. Independent appraisal is a sufficient protection against abuse.

"In Kansas we place the burden for valuation on the recipient agency or the museum . . . We require that the recipient receive public money, so if we do find a particular agency overvaluing works of art, we have some leverage over them through the grant of public funds."
—Kansas State Senator Ron Hein, author of the first state law restoring the fair market value deduction.

"On the federal level, the Collector of Internal Revenue reviews valuations placed on works of art that have been donated for income tax deductions. Conceivably you could incorporate that kind of provision in state legislation. The IRS appoints a special panel that rotates. It includes art historians, art dealers, museum people, artists, and it's been very tough. Since it has been in operation — and it has been six or seven years now — they've turned down a substantial number of claimed deductions for charitable gifts of art and have provided a feeling of security in the Collector's office that this issue is being handled properly."
— Stanford University Law Professor John Merryman

DEATH TAXES

RECOMMENDATION:
(1) Allow beneficiaries of artists' estates to defer death taxes, and/or
(2) allow the death tax to be paid with art as valued by the state death tax appraiser and delivered to an appropriate institution.

In 1965 sculptor David Smith was killed in an automobile accident. Between 1940 and 1963, his galleries had sold only 70 of his pieces, yielding Smith a gross income of $100,000 — an average of less than $5,000 a year. During the two years before his death, his fame increased, and his gallery sold five pieces for a total of $108,000 — more than his gross earnings for the previous 23 years.

However, at his home Smith left 425 unsold pieces, all subject to death taxes. Because of Smith's growing fame and his final sales, the Internal Revenue Service valued the sculpture at $5,256,918, an amount that would have created a federal estate tax liability of $2,444,629 and additional state inheritance taxes for his heirs. The estate had cash assets of little more than $200,000. Ultimately, a tax court compromised the value to $2,700,000.

The Smith case prompted painter Thomas Hart Benton to write: "The Feds have got it now so that just by comparing me with market values, they make me a multimillionaire on paper and I have got to pay taxes [on death] for which I have no money . . . the best solution would be to destroy all unsold works before I die."

In May 1976, 67-year-old Arizona artist Ted Degrazia, known worldwide for his portrayals of Southwest Indians, did just that. He transported an estimated $1,500,000 of his unsold paintings into the rugged Arizona mountains and burned them in protest of laws affecting artists' estates. Degrazia commented afterwards: "My heirs couldn't afford to inherit my works."

Several reforms have been proposed to remedy this situation, two of which the Arts Task Force recommends.

First, states could allow beneficiaries of artists' estates to defer death taxes, preferably until the art is sold. However, this approach assumes an uncertain event — the subsequent sale of the artwork. Alternatively, states could adopt existing federal law[1] that permits artists' estates to defer death taxes for five years and then pay the taxes in as many as ten annual installments at a low interest rate (4% in the federal code).

Michigan in 1980 became the first state to enact deferred payment legislation. The law allows a probate court judge to permit an artist's estate to defer inheritance tax interest free for up to 10 years.[2]

Deferred payment allows the estate to achieve maximum value through orderly liquidation of a portion of the art each year. It recognizes that artworks lack an inherent book value, that opportunities for sale generally are limited, and that art should be sold selectively rather than marketed immediately after the artist's death.

Second, states could allow the death tax to be paid with art as valued by the state death tax appraiser. In 1979 Maine became the first state to allow inheritance taxes to be paid with acceptable art.[3]

The new law requires the state museum commission to make a determination whether art offered to pay inheritance taxes is acceptable to the state. Acceptable art must be original or noteworthy, must advance understanding of Maine's fine art traditions or of the fine arts generally, or must contribute to the state's art collection. The commission and the estate's executor must agree on valuation, and the state tax assessor must review and accept the agreement. The measure also limits to $100,000 the value of art that the state may accept in any year, absent extraordinary circumstances or the willingness of the museum commission to reimburse the general fund for excess amounts. Art accepted in payment of death taxes becomes the property of the state museum.

"It is bothersome to me that the state can refuse to accept the art. Controversial art will not be accepted. The kind of art that will be accepted will be rather mediocre or non-controversial at that point in time. Controversial artists when they die may not be very acceptable, but they may be the cutting edge of that artform in the future."

—*Iowa Representative Robert Bina*

In recent years other states and the federal government have greatly increased death tax exemptions, and several states have repealed inheritance taxes. According to Colorado Representative Ronald Strahle, legislative discussion of artists' death taxes led in his state to a comprehensive examination and the ultimate repeal of Colorado's inheritance tax.

SUPPORTING POINTS

- Inheritance tax law requires that property be valued at fair market value at the date of death and that taxes be paid within months or at most a year after death. These provisions create a severe hardship for artists' estates in light of (1) the uniqueness of each artwork, (2) the tendency of artists to accumulate their art, (3) the knowledge that upon death an artist will produce no more work, (4) the volatile nature of the art market, and most importantly, (5) the inability of the market to absorb a large number of sales within a short time following the artist's death.

- *"America is losing thousands of valuable works of art each year as artists destroy their unsold works, rather than place an untold financial burden on their families.... [I]t is a national disgrace that our current tax system encourages the destruction of our cultural heritage. If this practice continues, future generations will be deprived of the pleasures of viewing contemporary American masterpieces."*

  —*New York Congressman Fred Richmond*

- Allowing death taxes to be paid with art solves the estate's problem of raising cash to pay the taxes and minimizes the possibility of the art's overvaluation by the inheritance tax appraiser or undervaluation by the estate's executors. Administration of these often complex estates will be greatly facilitated.

"The heirs of an estate in the State of Maine now have a choice. If they wish to pay the inheritance tax with works of art acceptable to the state, they may do so."

—*Maine Representative Merle Nelson*

NOTES

1. *Internal Revenue Code* Section 6166.
2. *Michigan Compiled Laws* Section 205.203.
3. See *Maine Revised Statutes* Title 27, Sections 91-93, and Title 36, Section 3688. Bills have been introduced in both houses of Congress incorporating the Maine provisions. S. 1078 (1979) was sponsored by former New York Senator Jacob Javits; HR. 7391 (1980), by Missouri Representative Richard Gephardt.

CONSUMER PROTECTION FOR PURCHASERS OF ART

Not surprisingly, the 1960's and 1970's boom in the sale of art occasioned a flood of forgeries and other fakes and, perhaps more importantly, inexpensive, photomechanical reproductions represented as original fine art prints and sold at high prices to unknowledgeable purchasers.

The Arts Task Force recommends two approaches in response to the proliferation of fraudulent and misrepresented art.

RECOMMENDATION #1:
Protect purchasers of fine art prints and other art issued in limited editions by requiring art dealers to disclose specific information regarding each piece sold.

California, Illinois, Maryland, New York, and Hawaii have enacted laws regulating the sale of fine prints. The chart on the following page sets forth each law's provisions.

Some of the problems not addressed by the present laws are: (1) they do not require disclosure of other relevant information, such as whether the print is a photomechanical reproduction, whether other artists were involved in making the print, and the seller's informational source; (2) some laws apply only to prints printed after their effective dates; (3) they do not cover other multiples, such as photographs and sculpture; (4) they do not require that buyers be informed of their legal remedies; and, most importantly, (5) they lack adequate enforcement mechanisms and consequently are largely ignored by dealers and printmakers.

SUPPORTING POINTS

● The dealer or printmaker usually knows much more about a fine print than does the purchaser. Therefore, the "let-the-buyer-beware" principle is especially unfair.

● The required information is easily obtained and disclosed to the purchaser, and disclosure is not required if the information is not available.

● Without this statutory protection, buyers have to prove either intent to defraud or breach of an express or implied warranty. With this protection buyers who discover that they have been misled will have to show only the lack of a written disclosure in order to rescind the contract and recover the purchase price.

● By discouraging proliferation of fakes and forgeries, the laws protect artists' reputations.

● Whether a print is actually signed by the artist's own hand is important to its value. Dealers have sometimes misled prospective purchasers by stating that a print is "signed" when in fact only the plate that produced the print had been signed. New York and Hawaii's laws specify that *signed* means by the artist's own hand.

FINE ART PRINT LAWS ENACTED THROUGH 1980

	CALIFORNIA (Civil Code Secs. 1740-1745)	**ILLINOIS** (Chapter 121½, Secs. 361-369)	**MARYLAND** (Commercial Law Title 14, Secs. 501-505)	**NEW YORK** (NY Gen. Bus. Law Secs. 228a-228e)	**HAWAII** Title 26, Sec. 481F
COVERAGE Date	Prints printed after July 1, 1971	Prints printed after July 1, 1972, and sold by noncreator	Prints printed after July 2, 1974	Prints sold after January 1, 1976 regardless of when printed	Prints sold after May 31, 1978, regardless of when printed
Value	Over $25 unframed Over $40 framed	Over $50 unframed Over $60 framed	Over $25 unframed Over $40 framed	Unlimited	Unlimited
PENALTY	Print's value + interest; three times value if willful violation.	Print's value + interest; three times value if willful violation + petty criminal offense with $1,000 maximum fine.	Print's value + interest; three times value if willful violation.	Print's value, damages, and criminal violation.	Print's value + interest; except greater of three times print's value or $1,000 if willful violation.
ENFORCEMENT	Within 1 year of discovery or 3 years of purchase.	Within 1 year of discovery or 3 years of purchase.	Within 1 year of discovery or 3 years of purchase	Not specified	Within 1 year of discovery or 3 years of purchase

REQUIRED WRITTEN INFORMATION	• name of artist
	• year printed
	• if limited edition:
	  ▪ no. signed or numbered
	  ▪ no. unsigned or unnumbered
	  ▪ no. any other proofs
	• status of plate
	• if other editions:
	  ▪ series no. of current editions
	  ▪ total size of all other editions
	• number of any prior states of same impression and relation to current edition
	• if posthumous or restrike edition and if plate reworked
	• name of printer
		• name of artist
		• year printed
		• type of print
		• total size of limited edition
		• status of plate
		• if other editions:
		  ▪ no. of editions
		  ▪ series no. of current edition
		• if posthumous or restrike edition and if plate reworked
		• name of printer
			• name of artist
			• year printed
			• if limited edition:
			  ▪ no. signed or numbered
			  ▪ no. unsigned or unnumbered
			  ▪ no. any other proofs
			• status of plate
			  ▪ no. total edition
			• if other editions:
			  ▪ series no. of current editions
			  ▪ total size of all other editions
			• number of any prior states of same impression and relation to current edition
			• if posthumous or restrike edition and if plate reworked
			• name of printer
				• Any alteration of the plates	• name of artist
					• year printed
					• if limited edition:
					  ▪ no. signed or numbered
					  ▪ no. unsigned or unnumbered
					  ▪ no. any other proofs
					• status of plate
					  ▪ no. total edition
					• if other editions:
					  ▪ series no. of current editions
					  ▪ total size of all other editions
					• number of any prior states of same impression and relation to current edition
					• if posthumous or restrike edition and if plate reworked
					• name of printer

OTHER PROVISIONS	• Seller may disclaim knowledge of any unavailable information. • Seller who describes print as a "reproduction" need not furnish other information unless the print is part of a limited edition.	• Seller may disclaim knowledge of any unavailable information. • Seller who describes print as a "reproduction" need not furnish other information unless the print is part of a limited edition.	• Seller may disclaim knowledge of any unavailable information. • Seller who describes print as a "reproduction" need not furnish other information unless the print is part of a limited edition.	• Seller may disclaim knowledge of any unavailable information. • Seller who describes print as a "reproduction" need not furnish other information unless the print is part of a limited edition. • "Signed" means by artist's own hand and signifies examination and approval by artist.	• Same as New York and California.

RECOMMENDATION #2:
Require art dealers to provide express warranties of genuineness with respect to the sale of limited edition prints and other artworks.

As further protection for art purchasers, the Arts Task Force recommends specific warranties of genuineness, an approach adopted by New York and Michigan.[1] The two nearly identical statutes provide that art dealers who sell to anyone other than another dealer and who furnish a written unqualified statement identifying the art's creator warrant that the work was created by that person. However, the laws also allow dealers to be more equivocating. If they choose not to warrant a work, they may "attribute" it to a particular artist, in which case no certainty exists that that person is the artist. Or they may indicate that the work is "of an artist's school," in which case it is not by that artist but rather by a pupil or close follower.

The two statutes also allow dealers to disclaim warranties, provided that the disclaimer specifically states that the seller assumes no risk, liability, or responsibility for the art's authenticity.

The laws' basic purpose is to eliminate questions about whether dealers' representations regarding authenticity are affirmative statements on which the purchaser may rely or mere opinions. The statutes recognize that buyers do rely on the art merchant's experience, education, and skill.

SUPPORTING POINTS

● Because many purchasers are not knowledgeable about authenticity, vast quantities of forgeries flood the market each year.[2] As between the dealer and purchaser, the former is in a better position to determine a piece's genuineness.

● The Uniform Commercial Code warranty provisions do not provide adequate protections for art buyers. The description "Picasso painting" may be interpreted as being merely in the manner or from the school of Picasso. Whether particular dealer representations legally become part of the transaction is unclear. Because the dealer may be puffing, the sales talk may or may not create a warranty. The UCC implied warranty provisions can easily be disclaimed. Specific state laws are therefore necessary to resolve these ambiguities peculiar to art.

● The laws are properly limited to art dealers and written statements and do not cover either transactions between collectors or oral representations.

NOTES
1. *New York General Business Law* Article 12-D, Sections 219-b to 219-e; *Michigan Compiled Laws* Sections 442.321-324.
2. There are other approaches for controlling art fraud and fakery. Some states have enacted specific criminal statutes relating to forgery and falsifying art authenticity certificates. See, for example, *New York Penal Law* Section 170.45, *New York General Business Law* Sections 219-h and 219-i; and *Maine Revised Statutes* Title 17-A, Section 705. The problem with these criminal statutes is that they require a prosecutor to show the faker's or seller's fraudulent intent — an extremely difficult task. See Bauman, Lawrence Scott, "Legal Control of the Fabrication and Marketing of Fake Paintings," 24 *Stanford Law Review* 930 (1972). Another possible although expensive approach is to create a national or state art registry, through which authenticity could be established.

How should the arts be structured within state government? Which approach is preferable: a single department encompassing all arts and culture programs, or a system of boards and commissions, or a combination of the two? Who should sit on state arts agency councils? The Arts Task Force offers two recommendations.

RECOMMENDATION #1:

Consider the feasibility and advisability of creating a state department to administer programs that may include some of or all the following: culture, arts, library, tourism, and humanities agencies.

Some states may place the department secretary or director on the governor's cabinet. When a state department is not feasible or advisable, program coordination among the various agencies should be encouraged.

In 1971 North Carolina became the first state to create a Department of Cultural Resources for administering state cultural programs. Five other states — Arkansas, Louisiana, Maine, South Dakota, and West Virginia[1] — and Puerto Rico have since followed North Carolina's lead and adopted a department structure encompassing cultural agencies. All place the department secretary or director on the governor's cabinet.

The agencies incorporated into each department vary. The chart below illustrates the differences.

"For North Carolina it [the cultural department structure] works, and it does make a difference for the quality of life of our state."

— North Carolina Representative Mary Seymour

DEPARTMENT DIVISIONS

NAMES OF DEPARTMENTS

Names of Departments	Arts or Arts and Humanities Agency	History and/or Archives	Historic or Cultural Preservation Agency	State Library	State Museum	Public Broadcasting Agency	State Symphony and/or State Music Conservatory	State Theatre or Theatre Companies	State Tourism Agency
Department of Arkansas Natural and Cultural Heritage	●	●	●		●				
Louisiana Department of Culture, Recreation, and Tourism	●			●	●	●			●
Maine Department of Educational and Cultural Services	●	●	●	●	●				
North Carolina Department of Cultural Resources	●	●	●	●	●		●	●	
Puerto Rico Arts and Culture Development Administration	●			●	●	●	●		
South Dakota Department of Education and Cultural Affairs	●		●	●	●				
West Virginia Department of Culture and History	●	●	●		●			●	

Utah is the only state that requires professional artist representation on the state's arts council, specifying one representative for each of eight different arts disciplines on the thirteen-member body. Many other states encourage the appointment of people with professional competence and experience in the arts. In contrast, Ohio requires that "at least a majority of the members of the council shall be persons other than professional artists."[2]

Utah has experienced positive results from its council composition. According to Assistant Director Arley Curtz, "We have people making policy who understand the arts."

According to Curtz, the problem of unrepresented arts disciplines and arts community components demanding "their" council positions has not arisen. "Other disciplines and components of the arts community are well represented on our 14 **advisory panels** that accomplish much of the nuts-and-bolts work of the council," Curtz said.

A 1966 National Endowment for the Arts survey of the 28 existing state arts agencies found only eight professional artists among the 196 council and commission members. Today, most states, while not mandating artist representation, do seat at least one professional artist.

SUPPORTING POINTS

● Cultural agencies will be more successful in seeking their annual operating budgets if they can act through the coordinated efforts of a department director.

● A department structure will enhance coordination of activities among cultural agencies, eliminating wasteful duplication of effort and infusing new ideas into each agency. Competition will be replaced by partnership, a change that will facilitate establishment of a statewide cultural network.

● Incorporating cultural activities into a state department will increase the importance of art and culture within state government, particularly if the secretary or director serves on the governor's cabinet.

OTHER CONSIDERATIONS

● A key question when a state cultural resources department is created is what will be the role of the formerly independent culture-related councils, boards, and commissions. Should these councils continue as the agency policy and decision makers or should the role become advisory to the department director and agency staff?

NOTES:
1. In 1981, Kentucky created a Department of the Arts by executive order.
2. See *Utah Code* Section 65-2-4 and *Ohio Revised Code* Section 3379.02. Other representative provisions are *New York Executive Law* Section 671(1), *Kansas Statutes* Section 74-5202, and *Idaho Code* Section 67-5602.

"The North Carolina Department of Cultural Resources with cabinet status brings the same political clout to the arts, archives and history, and library services as all other departments of state government."
— *Mary Seymour*

"I sit around the cabinet table every Monday morning with the rest of the appointed department heads . . . I have an equal voice with Human Resources which has 18,000 employees and millions more than we have in the budget."
— *Sara Hodgkins, North Carolina Secretary of Cultural Resources*

"In some instances the reorganization (into a cultural department) has strengthened the agencies and in some it has weakened them . . . We see the state art museum and state symphony emerging now as major cultural institutions. They've been strengthened by the reorganization."
— *Sara Hodgkins*

"I think a department of cultural resources is a much better solution than what has happened in states where a reorganization has occurred and the arts have been dispersed among a variety of departments, such as being buried in education or in other agencies where they lose their visibility."
— *Roy Helms, former Executive Director, National Assembly of State Arts Agencies; Executive Director, Consortium of Pacific Arts and Culture*

OTHER ISSUES

RECOMMENDATION:

Establish a state art bank through which the state, with the help of experts, purchases artwork by the state's artists to rent or loan for public display in public and private nonprofit facilities. Rental fees are used to purchase new art and for administrative expenses.

Alaska and Florida have established art banks, implemented as state arts agency programs and subject to annual appropriations included in agency budgets. (Most states' arts agency enabling laws permit establishing an art bank program without further legislation.)

Alaska's Art Bank has acquired more than 350 works, of which 95% are currently on loan to state agencies. The works, all portable, are placed in public view, primarily in state leased buildings where the state's percent-for-art program is inapplicable.

Beginning in 1981, Florida's Art Bank will place artworks in existing state buildings not eligible for percent-for-art acquisitions. The Art Bank will acquire works contributed by Florida artists awarded Fellowship Grants. The state plans to charge rental fees for artworks.

Other states have state art collections exhibited statewide. Most include annual purchases through artists' competition. Nebraska has the most comprehensive state art collection statute.[1]

The Canadian model, the world's most successful, embodies a banking concept:

An artist borrows money from the art bank, providing acceptable art as collateral for the loan. The art bank then rents the art for display by government and other designated agencies. The artist retains the right to repurchase the art at the original purchase price plus expenses and an administrative fee.[2] The artist also retains the copyright.

Since its 1972 inception the Canada Council's Art Bank has purchased more than 10,000 works from over 1,000 Canadian artists. The bank operates on a $1 million annual appropriation plus rental fees collected from minimum two-year leases to government agencies, hospitals, schools, and charities. (Museums may borrow without fee.) Three-person expert panels, hired by the bank, review slides from artists and galleries. Art is purchased at negotiated market value, subject to final approval by the Canada Council's visual arts officer. Not more than $23,000 worth of art may be purchased from an artist during any year. Quality is the only criterion for purchase.[3]

The Canadian Art Bank, not wanting to compete with commercial art dealers, does not rent purchased works to private individuals or corporations. Rentals are made at 12% of current value per year — an amount that includes shipping, insurance, and installation. Each year the Art Bank exhibits portions of the collection throughout the world and will lease outside Canada at a 24% annual rental. Art bank rental fees are accepted items in the budgets of various Canadian government agencies.

Four provincial art banks have been created as spin-offs of the national model.

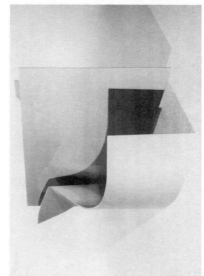

NOTES
1. See *Revised Statutes of Nebraska*, Sections 82-401 to 82-408.

2. The repurchase feature is unique to Canada's Art Bank. Proposed legislation to create an art bank for the United States, The National Art Bank Act of 1978, S. 2645 by New Jersey Senator Harrison Williams, would have allowed artists to repurchase but to retain only one-half of the profit upon resale with the other half retained by the art bank.

3. States considering establishment of an art bank should consider what has happened in Holland, where a 1956 artists' income maintenance program administered by the nation's welfare department now provides $40 million annually to some 2,500 Dutch visual artists. The government, through expert panels, commissions artists to create art or purchases already created works. The consensus is that most works are mediocre. Perhaps the system's main problem is that it was conceived and operates as a welfare program.

"Split", a painted aluminum sculpture, represents one of the more than 10,000 works purchased by the Canada Council Art Bank.

"One of the Art Bank's effects has been to strengthen the commercial art market in Canada. Eight years ago, the market for contemporary art was rather dismal. Now it has become considerably stronger."

— Christopher Youngs

SUPPORTING POINTS

● Art banks provide otherwise unavailable opportunities for artists, particularly those in rural and low-income communities.

● Publicly exhibited artworks purchased by art banks beautify public places.

● Public interest in art and cultural activities is heightened by this increased exposure to art.

● A properly administered art bank can be an efficient, cost-effective state government art program. Rental fees, if charged, defray administrative costs and provide funds for additional purchases.

● An art bank is an excellent way for a state to acquire a quality art collection.

● A state art bank complements a percent-for-art program by placing portable artworks in leased and existing state buildings.

● Providing artists a repurchase right allows them to realize the art's appreciated value and recognizes the lag time in public acceptance of art.

● State government art banks stimulate the state's private art market.

"The purpose of the art bank is not to make money but rather to expose people to art, educate people, and elevate the visual arts. If we do make money from rentals, it's just a nice bonus."

— Christopher Youngs, Director, Canada Council Art Bank

"We do not lease art, we loan it, and I think that is one of our strengths. If the government people had to pay a rental fee, we would not be as successful in loaning out the number of works as we have been. However, that policy may change."

— Christine D'Arcy, Visual Art Coordinator Alaska State Council on the Arts

"Culture is not inherited — it is acquired."

—Andre Malraux, French writer and Minister of Culture, 1958-1969

ARTISTS-IN-RESIDENCE

Among the most successful programs established by state arts agencies are those that employ professional artists in schools, communities, and social institutions. All 50 states and five special jurisdictions operate artists-in-schools programs, and most but not all also fund artists-in-communities and artists-in-social-institutions categories.

The National Endowment for the Arts' Artists-in-Schools program has received the greatest attention and funding. From beginnings in six states during 1969 and 1970, this program has expanded to include annually more than 3,300 artists in 7,300 schools reaching more than 1.5 million children. The program offers instruction in visual arts, crafts, design, theatre, dance, poetry, music, film and video, folk arts, architecture, and environmental arts.

Among the program's objectives are: (1) to incorporate the creative arts and artists into the school curriculum; (2) to enable participating children to gain respect for creativity in themselves and others and to understand creativity as an ongoing process; (3) to stimulate children through contact with producing professional artists; (4) to encourage children's lifelong involvement in the arts as participants and spectators; (5) to expand awareness of contemporary arts and of the artist's role in society; and (6) to enable participating artists to devote time and effort to their own creative work.

Students' evaluations often reveal that having artists in their classrooms has been the best experience of their school years. A 1977 program evaluation conducted by the Western States Arts Foundation found 93% of the teachers and administrators and 100% of artists and poets believe that

Artists-in-Schools has fostered students' creativity. High percentages also applauded cooperation between artists and teachers and replied positively when asked if they would participate in the program again.

Artists-in-communities places practicing professional artists with neighborhood community centers, art centers, and other local organizations in both urban and rural settings. Examples include a neighborhood or community center bringing an architect to work with people to explore and design a beautification project, a craftsperson conducting workshops in a senior citizen's center, or a theatre artist in a rural community developing productions as a form of self-expression for community members.

Placing artists in social institutions brings innovative and stimulating programming in the arts to hospitals, prisons, youth camps, geriatric homes, and psychiatric facilities. The basic purpose is to raise clients' levels of self-esteem through exposure to the creative process.

Poet Steven Ruffus assists a resident of a Salt Lake nursing home as part of an Artists-in-Community creative writing residency.

SUPPORTING POINTS

• Experiencing the arts is basic to the human spirit and thus should be available to all citizens. Artists-in-residence programs increase the visibility of the arts within the community and expand the role the arts play in clients' daily lives. Participants begin to perceive the arts as a creative process and not just as a product.

• Bringing professional artists into hospitals, retirement homes, prisons, and other institutions can have a habilitative, healing, or rehabilitative effect on residents. The programs facilitate self-expression and thereby enhance self-esteem.

• These programs showcase professional artists as dynamic and life-giving forces. Selected artists receive meaningful employment, often in an inspirational atmosphere conducive to their own artistic development.

• Employing resident artists is a relatively low-cost means of providing enriching, creative experiences to the public, especially in rural communities.

• Sharing and matching requirements are common to artist residency programs; as such, state funding of these programs stimulates local arts funding.

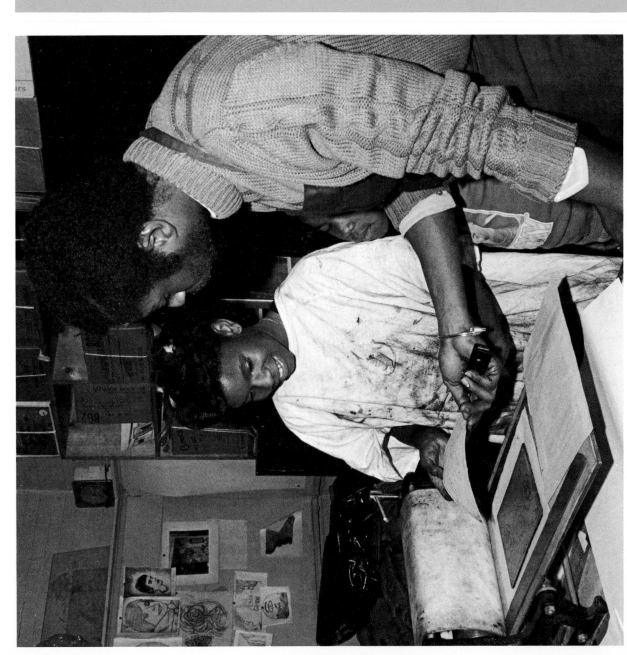

Students' evaluations often reveal that having artists in their schools has been the best experience of their school years.

46

DIRECT APPROPRIATIONS FOR ARTS INSTITUTIONS

RECOMMENDATION: Consider direct appropriations to major arts institutions either for specific capital expenditures or to provide a significant portion of the institution's budget. Such appropriations are in addition to the regular funding of the state arts agency.

The Arts Task Force's Survey of State Arts *Programs, Legislation, and Activities* reveals that 20 states provide direct appropriations for one or more of that state's major arts institutions.

The legislature funds these institutions through the line item (so called because it appears on a separate line in the annual budget) rather than through a state arts agency grant program. The legislature may make a small appropriation to pay for a specific capital project or a portion of the institution's operating budget.

Other states have appropriated funds and/or authorized state bonds to construct performing arts centers and other cultural facilities. Among notable examples:

- The new Tennessee Performing Arts Center in Nashville, which also includes an office tower and the State Museum, was built with $38 million in state bonds and $4.2 million in direct state funds.

- A 1979 Alaska statute authorizes both direct appropriations and state general obligation bonds to fund construction of cultural facilities with local government also contributing.[1]

- Washington State bonds provide matching funds for cultural facilities.

The line item is not without its critics. State arts agencies were established on the theory that a panel of experts free from political pressure can make appropriate, objective decisions about the allocation of arts funds. The agencies believe that the legislature should determine how much money should be allocated to, for example,

major arts institutions as a group, but that the agency should decide which institutions receive how much of that amount. The agencies are particularly upset when an institution is able to override its decision by successfully urging a legislator to sponsor a budget line item.

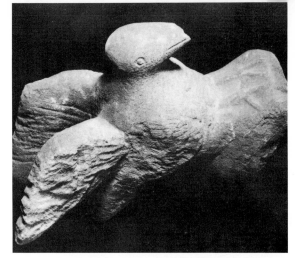

The new Tennessee Performing Arts Center (left) also includes a state office tower and the state museum, which houses works such as the 1790's printing press (above) and the sculpture "Bird" (below).

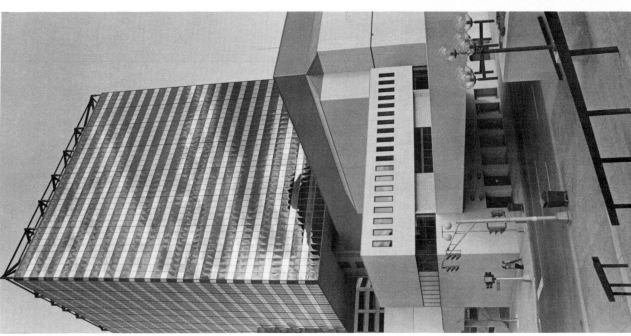

SUPPORTING POINTS

● Direct appropriations can supplement the state arts agency's budget. The result may be an increase in total arts funding.

● Direct appropriations can relieve the state arts agency of pressure to provide disproportionate funding to the state's highest quality arts institutions.

● Direct appropriations can be a more stable source of funding and can stimulate increased private contributions.

● Line items for arts institutions antedate most state arts agencies. Justification for these special appropriations often has been established over a period of years.

NOTES
1. *Alaska Statutes,* Section 43.18.500.

HISTORIC PRESERVATION

RECOMMENDATION:
Encourage legislation to provide both incentives and funding for the preservation of landmarks and properties that possess artistic, cultural, historic, or architectural significance.

Recognizing and preserving our country's architectural and historic heritage should parallel our dedication to advancing our cultural future. In each of our states and territories significant buildings once stood, buildings that are now remembered only by photographs. Entire districts of great historic value have been destroyed without consideration of their role in conveying a sense of our past.

Fortunately, the 1960's and 1970's have evidenced greater care in determining whether an attempt should be made to save deteriorating structures. This movement reflects an awareness of the charm, grace, character, and attention to detail missing from much of our newer buildings.

Sometimes an historic district can be an entire town such as Galesburg, Illinois or Georgetown, Colorado. In other cases — for example, Williamsburg, Virginia and Sturbridge, Massachusetts — communities have been restored to former splendor.

Preservation and restoration efforts can be economically important, both to government and the community. Sacramento, California is the first American city to use tax-increment financing to preserve and restore an historic district. At the project's beginning, the property tax base for the district was $500,000. Now, twenty years later, it is more than $8 million. Two-and-a-half-million tourists each year are expected to spend $20 million, bringing significant economic benefit to the community and additional tax revenues to state and local government.

This 1850 drawing and 1980 photograph of Charleston, South Carolina illustrate a successful program to preserve significant architectural, historic, and cultural resources.

"Preserving and restoring the best of our built heritage is one of the most important things we can do for future generations. It will give them a sense of place and a feeling for what life was like at a specific time. It will enhance their lives in the way that ours have been enriched — and add to cultural heritage."

— Minnesota State Senator
Emily Anne Staples

Restoration is on the average 30-40% less expensive than equivalent new construction, according to studies conducted by the President's Advisory Council on Historic Preservation. Moreover, the energy utilized to demolish existing buildings and to manufacture and erect new materials outweighs the energy savings from replacement buildings for periods of between 20 and 50 years.

"Support of historic preservation is economically beneficial, cost effective, and energy efficient. Preservation is not based on sentimentality, but on common sense."
— South Dakota State Senator Peg Lamont

Restoration projects provide employment opportunities, including jobs for trained artists and craftspeople, and in fact are much more labor intensive than new construction, according to the President's Advisory Council. The National Trust for Historic Preservation sponsors restoration training workshops.

The National Historic Preservation Act of 1966[1] created a federal-state historic preservation partnership. The Act funded a State Historic Preservation Officer for each state who may act to maintain that state's significant buildings and districts. For effective preservation, local and state officials, through coordinated efforts, must identify buildings or areas before they become endangered. This process, which

involves assessing and cataloging that which is worthy of preservation, is being undertaken in most states and in many communities. When appropriate, significant structures are being suggested for inclusion in the National Register of Historic Places. The following are recommendations for state action:

● **Enact state income tax benefits for preservation of officially designated historic buildings.**

State legislation could be modeled after a 1976 federal law[2] to provide income tax benefits for preservation or restoration of structures on the National Register of Historic Places. The tax benefits would be derived through rapid amortization and accelerated depreciation. This incentive would make renovation of historically significant buildings at least as financially attractive as is new construction.

"To achieve preservation of important structures, we need a broad range of legislation, such as accelerated depreciation and property tax abatement, and state historic preservation revolving funds for grants and loans, research, and long-range planning.
— Peg Lamont

● **Inventory state-owned buildings and evaluate their historic and architectural quality. Give priority to preserving the exteriors of buildings deemed significant and offer incentives to recycle interiors for contemporary state use.**

State policy to preserve culturally, historically, and architecturally significant state-owned structures needs to be revised and strengthened. In each state sound,

historic public buildings exist that can be recycled for contemporary uses as an alternative to constructing new facilities. This is an area that only a few states, including California, Minnesota, and Pennsylvania, have explored.

● **Provide state protection for National Historic Landmarks.**

"National Historic Landmark" is a federal designation for historic sites possessing national significance and is reserved for each state's most historically and architecturally significant structures. States should enact the strongest possible protective legislation for these structures and sites.

● **Establish and develop a state register of historic places.**

A state register should protect publicly-owned sites subject to state jurisdiction. An effective register will preserve sites from demolition, encroachment, and other adverse effects by requiring review of state funded projects. It also gives historic preservation a voice in the governmental discussions and decisions that weigh the advantages of new development against those of preserving the best of the old sites and structures. Minnesota's Historic Sites Act of 1965[3] predated the National Register of Historic Places. North Carolina and South Dakota have established state registers that incorporate structures and sites listed in the National Register.[4]

● **Fund grants to identify significant buildings in smaller communities.**

The small community is in urgent need of professional help and guidance. Federal preservation programs increasingly favor urban areas. States should fill this vacuum and provide technical assistance to determine which historic places in these rural communities should and can be preserved.

Historic preservation is compatible with new development. Through a coordinated effort with careful planning, we can successfully protect existing historic structures and, at the same time, develop new facilities, including some that will have future architectural and historic significance.

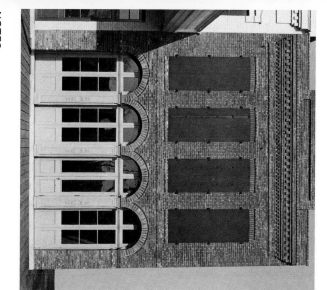

NOTES
1. *United States Code*, Title 16, Sections 470-470 (b).
2. *United States Code*, Title 26, Section 191.
3. *Minnesota Statutes*, Sections 138.51 and following.
4. *North Carolina General Statutes*, Sections 121-12 and South Dakota Statutes, Chapter 1-19A.

RECOMMENDATION:
Simplify initial applications and annual reporting requirements for small arts organizations filing for state nonprofit, tax-exempt status.

A problem most acute to small, volunteer-staffed, nonprofit arts organizations is the initial and annual state reporting requirements necessary to incorporate and to gain and maintain nonprofit, tax-exempt status. The hundreds and sometimes thousands of dollars in legal, accounting, and filing fees can make the difference between continued existence and dissolution. The many hours that volunteers must spend filling out forms and records are so trying that only the most dedicated continue to serve.

The Arts Task Force recognizes that the state government agencies charged with policing nonprofit organizations that solicit and receive public funds are performing an important public service. However, the Task Force believes that with respect to nonprofit arts organizations operating on small budgets, the public benefit must be balanced against the burden the substantial filing requirements place on these groups. For example, a community orchestra in a rural township receives several thousand dollars in annual grants and donations to support its services, but must spend long hours and a significant percentage of its funding to secure and continue its nonprofit, tax-exempt classification. State legislatures should consider whether the need to protect against potential abuse is well served.

LOCAL ARTS FUNDING

RECOMMENDATION:

(1) Allow local governments to institute a hotel-motel occupancy tax or other taxes to fund cultural and tourism-related institutions and events. (2) Authorize local governments to provide funding for arts performances such as operas, symphonies, concerts, theatre, and dance, for art exhibitions, and for a percent-for-art program for local public buildings and facilities.

"The hotel-motel tax helps fund the arts organizations in San Francisco that help make it the kind of place you want to visit. It is a sensible and logical form of taxation."

—Richard LeBlond, President, San Francisco Ballet, and President, California Confederation of the Arts

In most states, enactment of a local hotel-motel occupancy tax or other taxes to fund cultural and tourism activities requires a state enabling act. According to the Arts Task Force survey, fourteen states have enacted laws authorizing locally imposed hotel-motel occupancy taxes, also commonly referred to as transient-occupancy or bed taxes.[1] In some states the enabling law requires that the city or county spend all (Illinois, Louisiana, Michigan, Texas, Utah, and Washington) or a specific portion (Iowa and New Mexico) of the tax receipts on tourism and the arts. In others, such as Georgia, the authorizing act mandates that the local government spend an unspecified portion of the tax income for that purpose.

Transient occupancy taxes vary from 1% to 10%. Some laws establish a maximum percentage; Michigan at 5%; Texas at 4%, and Washington at 2%. Nebraska's law authorizes a 2% local occupancy tax for local tourism promotion and also funds state government tourism activities through a 1% sales tax on hotel accommodations.

The U.S. Department of Commerce reports that in 1977 the hotel-motel occupancy tax was second only to general revenues as the largest source of support for local arts and tourism promotion.[2] Other sources include entertainment taxes, mixed drink taxes, and earmarked sales taxes. Aspen, Colorado has allocated a portion of its real-estate transfer tax to the arts, and in Boulder, the city council allocated 1% of the 1979 budget to arts support. This percentage was increased for 1980.

Several states, including Illinois and Ohio, have authorized local ballot measures to

impose increased property taxes with revenues earmarked for the arts.[3] Among unusual state enabling laws is Florida's statute authorizing use of local government dog and horse racing revenues for the arts.[4]

Other state laws specifically authorize local governments to fund the arts. Some are directed toward the creation and funding of local arts agencies,[5] others allow the funding of arts performances and exhibitions,[6] and still others permit local percent-for-art programs for public buildings and places.[7]

Gerald Walburg's "Indo Arch" was commissioned under Sacramento, California's 2%-for-art ordinance.

SUPPORTING POINTS

- Cultural activities are major attractions for tourists and conventioneers. Using transient-occupancy taxes to support these activities is appropriate.

- Hotel-motel occupancy taxes also fund visitor and convention bureaus necessary for the maintenance and growth of this important industry.

- Imposition of local taxes to support cultural and tourism activities is part of the public-private partnership essential to attract visitors.

- Supporting cultural resources through local taxes directed at tourists also helps make these resources available to the entire community.

- Cultural opportunities are important to businesses in determining where to locate. Encouraging the arts through local tax revenues makes good economic sense.

- Tourism dollars generate additional tax revenue for local government. Supporting tourist and arts promotion with public funds will attract more tourists.

NOTES

1. See *Arizona Revised Statutes*, Section 42-1314B; *California Revenue and Taxation Code*, Section 7280; *Georgia Code*, Title 91A, Chapter 62 (Sections 91A-6201 and following); *Illinois Statutes*, Chapter 24, Sections 8-3-13 and 8-3-14; *Indiana Statutes*, Title 6, Article 9, Chapters 1-5 (authorizes specific counties to impose an occupancy tax); *Iowa Code*, Section 422A.2.4a; *Kentucky Revised Statutes*, Section 83.350 and Section 5 of House Bill 858 (1980); *Louisiana Statutes*, Section 33:27711.3. (New Orleans only); *Michigan Statutes*, Section 5.3194(361) and following; *New Mexico Statutes*, Section 3-38-13 and following; *Texas Civil Statutes*, Article 1269j-4.1; *Utah Code* Title 17-31-2; *Virginia Code* Sections 58-76.1 and 58-76.2 (Arlington County and cities therein); and *Revised Code of Washington*, Section 67.28.180 and following.

2. *City Government, Tourism and Economic Development* — *Volume 1*, Washington, United States Department of Commerce (September 1978).

3. See *Illinois Statutes*, Chapter 24, Section 11-45.1-1 and following; and *Ohio Revised Code*, Section 3381.01 and following.

4. *Florida Statutes*, Section 550.03.

5. See, for example, *Florida Statutes*, Section 265.32.

6. See, for example, *Utah Code*, Title 17-15-21.

7. See, for example, *Texas Code*, Title 20, Article 601b, Section 5.19.

BIBLIOGRAPHY

PERCENT-FOR-ART IN PUBLIC PLACES

Berkowitz, Rhoda L., "The One Percent Solution: A Legislative Response to Public Support for the Arts," 10 *Toledo Law Review* 124 (1978).

Green, Dennis, *% For Art: New Legislation Can Integrate Art and Architecture*, Denver, Western States Arts Foundation (1976).

Harney, "The Proliferating One Percent Programs for the Use of Art in Public Buildings," *American Institute of Architects Journal* 35 (1976).

THE ARTS IN EDUCATION

General References

The Arts, Education and Americans Panel, *Coming to Our Senses*, New York, McGraw-Hill Book Company (1977).

Bloom, Kathryn, et al, *An Arts in Education Source Book*, New York, The JDR 3rd Fund (1980).

Perkins, David, "Theory in Arts Education: The Pound of Feathers and the Pound of Lead," 11 *Journal of Aesthetic Education* 5 (January 1977).

Summit Conference on the Arts and Education, Washington, D.C., Alliance for Arts Education (1980).

Report of the Task Force on the Education, Training and Development of Professional Artists and Arts Educators, Washington, D.C., National Council on the Arts and the National Endowment for the Arts (December 1978).

Arts in Basic Education

Barzun, Jacques, and Saunders, Robert J., *Art in Basic Education*, Washington, D.C., Council for Basic Education (1979).

Eddy, Junius, "Art Education: The Basics and Beyond," 30 *Art Education* 6 (November 1977).

Comprehensive State Planning for the Arts in Education: A Survey of the Current Status of State Arts Education Plans and Programs, Washington, D.C., Alliance for Arts Education (1979).

In-Service Teacher Training

Barr-Johnson, Virginia, "What Can a Teacher Gain from In-Service Activities?" 32 *Art Education* 13 (January 1979).

Engel, Martin, "The Continuing Education of Teachers of the Arts," 29 *Art Education* 4 (September 1976).

Koznin, Allan, "The Lincoln Center Institute," 7 *Stagebill* 6 (September 1979).

Gifted and Talented

Someone's Priority, Denver, Colorado Department of Education (1979).

Education of Gifted and Talented Pupils, California State Department of Education (1979).

Schools for the Arts

The North Carolina School of the Arts: A Vision in Motion, Winston-Salem, The North Carolina School of the Arts Foundation.

ARTISTS' RIGHTS

Artist-Art Dealer Relations

Comment, "Regulation of the New York Art Market: Has the Legislature Painted Dealers Into a Corner?" 46 *Fordham Law Review* 939 (1978).

Sandison, Hamish, *Artists and Galleries: A Guide to the New California Artist-Dealer Relations Law*, San Francisco, Bay Area Lawyers for the Arts (1975).

Artists' Live-Work Space

Lehmann, Phyllis, and Fain, Kenneth, "Staying Aloft," *Cultural Post*, National Endowment for the Arts, Issue 23:1 (May-June 1979).

Mann, Mary Sullivan, *The Right to Housing: Constitutional Issues and Remedies in Exclusionary Zoning*, New York, Praeger Publishers (1976).

Schulman, Wendy, "SoHo: A Victim of its Own Success," *New York Times*, Section 8 (Real Estate) (November 24, 1974).

Shapiro, Andrew O., "Legal Lowdown on Converting Loft Buildings," 11 *New York Magazine* 65 (April 17, 1978).

Skites, Jacqueline, and Raikein, Laurin, "Where Do Artists' Live and Work?" *Art Worker News* (December 1974-January 1975) part I, page 1. (February 1975) part II, page 1.

Art Preservation

Comment, "Copyright: Moral Right — A Proposal," 43 *Fordham Law Review* 793 (1975).

Merryman, John, "The Refrigerator of Bernard Buffet," 27 *Hastings Law Journal* 1023 (1976).

Rose, Diana, "Calder's Pittsburgh: A Violated and Immobile Mobile," 77 *ARTnews* 38 (January 1978).

Weil, Stephen E., "The 'Moral Right' Comes to California," 78 *ARTnews* 88 (December 1979).

Resale Royalties

Bongartz, Roy, "Writers, Composers and Actors Collect Royalties — Why Not Artists?" *New York Times*, February 2, 1975, Section 2, at 1.

Crawford, Tad, "Legislation: Art Resale Proceeds Rights," 43 *American Artist* 82 (July 1979).

Price, Monroe, "Government Policy and Economic Security for Artists: The Case of the Droit de Suite," 77 *Yale Law Journal* 1333 (1968).

Price, Monroe E., and Sandison, Hamish, *A Guide to the California Resale Royalties Act*, San Francisco, Bay Area Lawyers for the Arts (1976).

Schulder, "Art Proceeds Act: A Study of the Droit de Suite and a Proposed Enactment for the United States," 61 *Northwestern University Law Review* 19 (1966).

TAX LEGISLATION

Artists' Income Tax Deductions

Baldwin, Carl R., "Art Money: Acting to Reform the Tax Reform Act," 64 *Art in America* 40 (May-June 1976).

Beghe, Renato, "The Artist, the Art Market, and the Income Tax," 29 *Tax Law Review* 491, at 514-523 (1974).

Rosenbaum, Lee, "More on Tax Reform: Artists Strike Out," 64 *Art in America* 23 (November-December 1976).

Hearings on the Subject of Tax Reform Before the House Committee on Ways and Means, 93d Congress, 1st Session, Part 15 (1973).

Death Taxes

Behrenfeld, William, "Should Artists Receive Special Tax Consideration?" 43 *American Artist* 12 (May 1979).

Cochrane, Diane, "The Artist and His Estate Taxes," 38 *American Artist* 32 (January 1974).

Sloane, Leonard, "Valuing Artist's Estates: What is Fair? 75 *ARTnews* 91 (April 1976).

CONSUMER PROTECTION FOR ART PURCHASERS

Fine Art Print Disclosure

Chamberlain, Betty, "Prints: Can We Legislate?" 40 *American Artist* 26 (April 1976).

Duffy, Robert E., Jr., "Disclosure Requirements in Connection With the Sale of Fine Art Prints," 48 *California State Bar Journal* 528 (1973).

Pollock, "Art Print Legislation in California: A Critical Review," 25 *Stanford Law Review* 586 (1973).

Wayne, June, & Sandison, Hamish, "On Print Disclosure Legislation," 40 *American Artist* 58 (April 1976).

Warranties of Genuineness

DuBoff, Leonard D., "Controlling the Artful Con: Authentication and Regulation," 27 *Hastings Law Journal* 973 (1976).

Hodes, Scott, "Wanted: Art Legislation for Illinois," 51 *Illinois Bar Journal* 218 (1968).

Note, "Uniform Commercial Code Warranty Solutions to Art Fraud and Forgery," 14 *William & Mary Law Review* 409 (1972).

OTHER ISSUES

Art Banks

Bongartz, Roy, "Banking Art in Ottawa," 76 *ARTnews* 80 (April 1977).

Lewis, Jo Ann, "Cashing in on the Art Bank," *Washington Post* November 20, 1977, Section F, Page 1.

McConathy, Dale, "Art Bank," XXXII *Artscanada* 1 (Autumn 1975).

Hearings Before the Committee on Human Resources, United States Senate, 95th Congress, 2nd Session, on S. 2645, the National Art Bank Act of 1978; August 22 and 23, 1978. Washington, United States Government Printing Office (1978).

Artists-In-Residence

Bergin, Thomas P., and Martin, Kathryn, "An Artists-in-Schools Program Puts Joy in Education," 44 *The Education Digest* 53 (January 1979).

Patrick, Barry M., "The 'Artist' in Education," 79 *Design* 30 (January/February 1978).

Historic Preservation

Kettler, Ellen L., and Reams, Bernard D., *Historic Preservation Law: An Annotated Bibliography*, Washington, D.C., Preservation Press of the National Trust (1975).

Morrison, Jacob H., *Historic Preservation Law*, Washington, D.C., Preservation Press of the National Trust (1974).

Guidelines for State Historic Preservation Legislation, Washington, D.C., U.S. Advisory Council on Historic Preservation (1972).

The Economic Benefits of Preserving Old Buildings, Washington, D.C., Preservation Press of the National Trust (1976).

Local Arts Funding

Kreisberg, Luisa, *Local Government and the Arts*, New York, American Council for the Arts (1979).

Tourism USA: Volume IV — Sources of Assistance. Washington, D.C., United States Department of Commerce (1978).

The Council of State Governments, *Tourism: State Structure, Organization, and Support*, Washington, D.C., United States Department of Commerce (1979).

ADVOCATING THE ARTS IN STATE LEGISLATURES

In recent years, legislators supportive of the arts have joined with artists, arts administrators, culturally interested citizens, and local and state arts council members to argue successfully for increased arts agency budgets and for passage of state arts legislation. Although advocates of state support for the arts until recently have not been as experienced in lobbying as other interest groups, they are now quickly learning methods of winning greater state funding for the arts.

What are these successful advocacy approaches? The following discussion explores four approaches and outlines a variety of strategies utilized in six states. The section also discusses committee structures that legislatures have established to consider arts-related issues and to interact with state arts agencies.

Some successful Broadway shows began as state-funded off Broadway productions, such as Albert Innaurato's "Gemini". (See The Economic Impact Approach, page 56.)

Aesthetically pleasing architecture represents a higher value in our lives. (See Aesthetic Considerations, page 62.)

The American public's attendance at arts presentations is growing rapidly. Above, the Paul Taylor Dance Company presents "Airs". (See Public Support for the Arts, page 59.)

APPROACHES TO ARTS ADVOCACY

conscious legislators that allocating more money for the arts makes good sense.

More frequently in recent years arts advocates have cited the arts' beneficial economic impact in arguing for increased state arts appropriations.

The economic argument is most often presented in the context of a multiplier effect: Every dollar spent by an arts institution, artist or arts audience, or every state dollar allocated to the arts, generates **X** dollars in economic impact within the community through successive rounds of spending, results in **X** jobs, and returns **X** dollars to government in tax revenue.

A related approach, which links the arts and tourism, is based on the fact that much of the potential economic impact of the arts results from the tourist multiplier.

One of the most successful efforts directly connecting the arts and tourism is the "I Love New York" advertising campaign, which promotes Broadway theatre nationwide and to which New York State has appropriated over $9 million each year since 1976.

Tourism, which had experienced no real growth for five years before the 1976 campaign and which had slipped to the number two New York industry, rebounded to first place immediately following the initial advertising campaign. Theatre attendance, which had been steadily declining, skyrocketed. For example, during the eight-month period from January to August, 1978, the campaign resulted in the sale of an estimated 530,000 additional Broadway theatre tickets, producing an economic impact in direct and indirect spending of $23 million.

The economic approach has obvious appeal, especially in convincing budget-

Numerous studies were conducted during the 1970's to demonstrate the beneficial economic effects that the arts produce. These studies are included as part of this chapter's bibliography. On the following page are findings from some of the most methodologically precise studies.

THE ARTS AND THE NEW ENGLAND ECONOMY

This was a 1978 study of 2,830 cultural organizations.

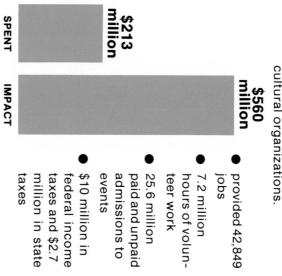

$213 million SPENT

$560 million IMPACT

- provided 42,849 jobs
- 7.2 million hours of volunteer work
- 25.6 million paid and unpaid admissions to events
- $10 million in federal income taxes and $2.7 million in state taxes

THE IMPACT OF ARTISTIC AND CULTURAL ACTIVITIES ON CONNECTICUT'S ECONOMY, 1975

This study measured the direct and indirect impact of 81 Connecticut cultural institutions.

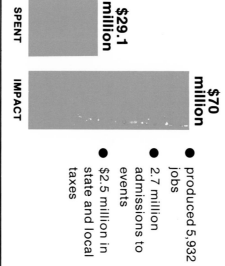

$29.1 million SPENT

$70 million IMPACT

- produced 5,932 jobs
- 2.7 million admissions to events
- $2.5 million in state and local taxes

THE ECONOMIC IMPACT OF ARTS AND CULTURAL INSTITUTIONS: A MODEL FOR ASSESSMENT AND A CASE STUDY IN BALTIMORE

This is one of the most detailed and precise studies to date. It examined the fiscal 1976 impact of eight Baltimore arts institutions. The eight received $2.3 million in government funding.

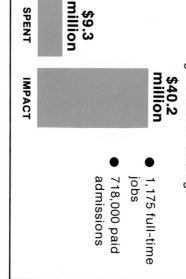

$9.3 million SPENT

$40.2 million IMPACT

- 1,175 full-time jobs
- 718,000 paid admissions

While the studies **do** indicate that the arts have a positive result on the regional, state, or local economy, overemphasizing the economic impact argument has several drawbacks. First and most importantly, it depreciates the arts' aesthetic value and basis.

"As a businessman and investor, I'm very tempted to embrace 100 percent the notion that... the economic influence of the arts is so profound as to justify your own states' increased appropriations of considerable size. I would not be doing you an injustice and I said that... The first reason to talk of advancing support for the arts is that,

just as with health and education, the arts represent an example of a civilized society to be enjoyed by its people and their children and grandchildren."
—Martin Segal, President, Cultural Assistance Center, New York City

Another problem is that the value of the economic impact studies, even those that are firmly based methodologically, can be overemphasized. *The Arts in the Economic Life of the City* succinctly summarizes the studies' limitations:

[The economic impact studies] put the arts in the same mold as every other activity that involves various rounds of expenditures.[1]

This study, conducted by the Urban Innovations Group of the UCLA School of Architecture and Urban Planning under the direction of Dean Harvey S. Perloff, also suggests a different economic justification for state arts support. As Dr. Perloff told the Arts Task Force in November, 1978:

The country is going to become very dependent on the arts in the future. Manufacturing will no longer employ very many people — we will be lucky to maintain the present level in absolute numbers. Already 70% of all employment is in services and the proportion is increasing. Tourism combined with the arts is becoming one of the most important industries in the United States.

businesses, and that, like education and medicine, deserve special priority when government funding decisions are made. And advocates should also consider the other approaches that follow.

Jazz artists Dizzy Gillespie (right) and Jon Faddis (left).

NOTES
1. Perloff, *The Arts in the Economic Life of the City*, at page 5.
2. *Ibid*, at page 10.

The Arts in the Economic Life of the City advocates using the arts as a means of economic development and revitalization, particularly in the central city area.

The arts can contribute to the economic revitalization of downtown areas and older neighborhoods of the city and region; to the enlargement of tourism, the convention trade, and other attractions (and their attendant expenditures); and in general, to the economic viability of urban communities.²

The book argues that the arts meet employment and income needs of the central city's poorer population and thus contribute to community cohesion. It recommends creating artists' enclaves, using artists as dynamic city builders, and injecting a cultural element into local planning. It suggests maximizing arts employment by tying the arts to various public services, such as arts therapy, arts education, and art in public places, and by including the arts as part of urban redevelopment and preservation.

Dr. Perloff's book also places the arts within a limited category of services—for example, medicine and education—that are funded only partially by direct payments. These services are deemed to have a societal value that merits a special claim on the community's wealth and income. Therefore, part of the cost of producing these services is met through government funding and other supportive policies.

Another important developmental use of the arts is attracting business and industry to an area. Martin Segal, at the May, 1979 Task Force meeting made the point well.

"Every state wants to have business, wants to keep the businesses that are there and attract others, and wants to keep the economy and the life of the state attractive to its citizenry. Because when a state is not attractive to its business and citizenry, they do what was started in this country a long time ago. They go elsewhere. They move. So your state legislatures have a first class reason for making life appealing in that state. And if your state is interested in raising the level of your people, it must be interested in the arts.... We should look at appropriations for the arts as investments in the present and the future."

Perhaps the most important economic argument in favor of state arts support is that the arts in reality permeate our lives. While our society has tended to talk about the arts as a frill, the arts are in fact central to our daily lives. Although we may not recognize it, the arts are a vital part of our most important industries. Their influence is found in the architecture and interior design of our homes and offices, in the design of the clothes we wear, the automobiles we drive and the appliances we use, and in the advertising of consumer goods and services. The arts also are at the very core of our vast commercial entertainment complex—radio, television, motion pictures, and recordings. The lifestyle that we have come to appreciate is very much dependent on the arts.

In summary, if resort to economic impact figures is necessary to support additional appropriations for the arts, ample evidence exists to substantiate their economic value. However, in presenting economic arguments, arts advocates should also point out that the arts are an increasingly important service industry that can play a substantial economic development role, that can help to revitalize decaying urban areas, that can provide jobs and attract

One of the most compelling arguments for state arts support and funding is the public's willingness to increase taxes to pay for that support. Results of a 1980 Harris opinion poll, *Americans and the Arts*,[1] reveal that, at a time when many Americans oppose increased taxes and government spending, a major-

ity of taxpayers would support some increase in taxes to fund the arts. Because total federal and state arts funding for fiscal 1980-81 averaged only slightly more than $1 per person, a program to increase government arts dollars *tenfold* would continue to receive support from most Americans.

A majority of those surveyed believe that government should assist arts organizations needing help, and that the arts are not self-supporting and are dependent on both public and private contributions. A majority also favor an incentive plan to stimulate private donations to the arts.

FUNDING:

● Would you be willing to pay more tax money each year to fund the arts?

	$25 more	$15 more	$10 more	$5 more
YES	51%	59%	65%	70%
NO	45%	39%	33%	28%

● Should the federal government assist arts organizations needing help?

50% YES

45% NO

● State government?

60% YES

37% NO

● County and municipal government?

64% YES

31% NO

● Do you favor an incentive plan to stimulate private donations? ($1 government/$3 private source matching plan)

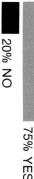

59% FAVOR

36% OPPOSE

PERCEPTIONS:

Other poll findings indicate that the arts are perceived in a clearly positive light.

● How do you perceive the arts? The arts are:

"A positive experience in a troubled world"

75% AGREE

19% DISAGREE

"A source of creative expression and experience that is rare"

70% AGREE

25% DISAGREE

"An uplift from everyday experiences"

75% AGREE

22% DISAGREE

"Pure pleasure to experience or participate in"

80% AGREE

16% DISAGREE

EDUCATION:

The Harris poll also shows clear public support for inclusion of the arts in the basic education curriculum.

● Should school children be exposed to the arts and cultural events?

93% YES

7% NO

● Should arts courses be included in school budgets?

75% YES

20% NO

● Should arts courses be taught for full academic credit?

75% FOR CREDIT

22% NOT FOR CREDIT

With this evidence, school administrators and legislators should realize that the public does not favor cutting back on school arts programs and considers the arts to be an integral and important part of public education.

Individual participation in a view camera work-shop indicates the increasingly vital role the arts play in each American's life.

The Harris study indicates not only an increased interest but also a growing involvement and participation in the arts.

The 1980 poll, when compared with a similar 1975 study,[2] shows a sharp upward trend in attendance at almost every type of arts presentation. More people are viewing movies, theatre, live musical and/or dance presentations, and museum exhibits than were in 1975. Moreover, the 1980 survey shows a striking rise in the level of personal participation in the arts over the past five years.

These results are convincing evidence of public support for the arts.

"The arts are becoming a more vital and integral part of the mainstream of American life."
—Louis Harris and Associates, 1980

NOTES:

1. Louis Harris, *Americans and the Arts*, New York, American Council for the Arts (1980).
2. Louis Harris, *Americans and the Arts*, New York, American Council for the Arts (1975).

GOVERNMENT ARTS SUPPORT—AN HISTORICAL PERSPECTIVE

Although government arts funding is relatively new to this country, it has existed for centuries in other parts of the world. In fact, where the arts have flourished, they often have been sustained by public authority.

In ancient Greece, for example, Plato prescribed art as essential to the education of the ideal citizen, and Aristotle urged the state to teach its members art for the appropriate use of their leisure. The city-state responded by providing cultural activities, such as festivals, dramatic performances, and sacred ceremonies as a public service. The art of the Parthenon was a direct charge on the treasury of Athens.

In fifteenth century Italy, artists emerged as honored citizens who were supported by the state. At the height of the Renaissance, Florence flourished under Lorenzo de' Medici, who gathered artists and philosophers in his court and staged public pageants for the citizenry. The Papacy, which enjoyed a secular political role during that period, also supported the arts. Many paintings by Michelangelo and by Raphael were created with the Church's patronage.

In Britain, government support for arts institutions dates from the early nineteenth century. The British government has funded the National Gallery since 1823, the British Museum since 1843, the Victoria and Albert Museum since 1852, and the Tate Gallery since 1892. Twentieth century government-funded arts institutions include the BBC (1927) and the British Film Institute (1933).

During the post-World War II period the modern democratic governments have served as promoters, stimulators, and financers of the arts. Most European governments have cultural ministries with the same cabinet-level status as education, health, finance, and defense in their parliamentary structures. Perhaps the most exemplary contemporary government arts funding is found in West Berlin, where the annual appropriation to the arts is approximately $220 million, equal to $110 per capita for that city's two million people!

In the United States, Utah created the first state arts commission in 1899 and Minnesota the second in 1902. The Utah Art Institute received $2,000 for the first biennium; the Minnesota State Art Society administered an annual $7,000 appropriation until World War I. By 1932, thirty-three states were supporting the arts by providing financial aid or building space.

Most Americans are familiar with the federal art programs of the 1930's, especially the Works Progress Administration (WPA) Art Project. However, the WPA was only one of four federal agencies administering programs to employ artists and to bring art to the people. These programs were of particular benefit to rural citizens, an estimated 90% of whom had never had the opportunity to see or study original works of art.

Current government support for the arts dates from the 1965 founding of the National Endowment for the Arts (which was established at the same time as the National Endowment for the Humanities). Federal policy and appropriations have stimulated the states to fund the arts. State appropriations have grown from $1.9 million in 1965 to $111.7 million for 1981.

"Orpheus" by Gerhard Marcks, located at the University of Houston.

AESTHETIC CONSIDERATIONS

Although government arts support can be justified by the arts' economic impact, by the polls showing that the public favors government funding, and by citing historic examples of government support, the arts' greatest value lies in their potential for enriching each individual's life.

The arts represent creativity, growth, imagination, and a positive force in our lives; they symbolize the perfection of self-discipline and offer an opportunity to enhance self-esteem; they enable us to recall past experiences, and they thrust us into the future; they open and expand our vision and create responses that draw on our emotions; they enable us to utilize our senses and, through sensory experiences, to appreciate colors, sounds, shapes, movements, and even tastes and smells. The arts also provide a common language and means of understanding that can help to bring different people and cultures together.

We are also motivated toward great literature, music, theatre, dance, paintings, sculpture, architecture, crafts, and films by our realization that these artforms represent a higher value — that they nourish the spirit of both the artist and the audience, that they facilitate the appearance, perception, and appreciation of beauty in our lives. As Plato stated in *The Republic*, "from the love of the beautiful, has sprung every good in heaven and earth."

In supporting the arts, it may at first appear politically prudent to overlook the aesthetic argument. Legislators and other advocates may feel uncomfortable presenting the arts from the perspective of beauty and cultural enrichment. Yet, every legislator has personally experienced some impact from the arts and will respond from his or her own experiences.

"The arts are a common denominator providing a universal language that all participants can appreciate. Further development of the arts in the Southern region will mold an even stronger heritage for future generations."

— Alabama State Senator Ted Little

"The arts are more than enjoyment for the viewer. They provide the opportunity to delve into one's own personality and character as a means of discovery and fulfillment of one's wishes and dreams. The arts aid people's lives and do more for the poor, handicapped, and downtrodden than many of our social programs."

— Wisconsin Representative Dismas Becker

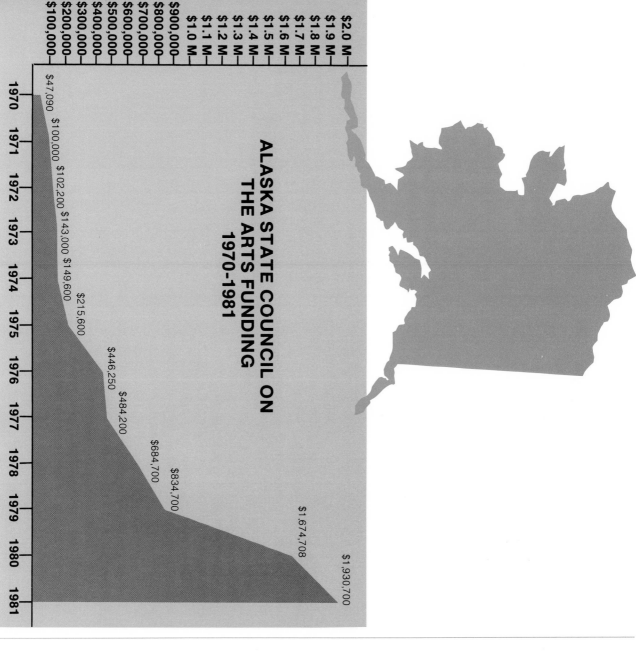

**ALASKA STATE COUNCIL ON
THE ARTS FUNDING
1970-1981**

1970	$47,090
1971	$100,000
1972	$102,200
1973	$143,000
1974	$149,600
1975	$215,600
1976	$446,250
1977	$484,200
1978	$684,700
1979	$834,700
1980	$1,674,708
1981	$1,930,700

ALASKA

During the 1970's, state funding for the arts in Alaska experienced steady growth at the same time that state government attempted to restrict spending and bureaucratic expansion. In fact, during this period little support existed for any program development that required additional dollars or more state employees.

The increase in funding resulted from strategies that the Alaska State Council on the Arts incorporated to overcome the general resistance to growth in government. Specifically, the Council stressed the following principles:

● Inflation was a reality for both grantees and state government, and the Council therefore convinced budget analysts to allow, as an annual automatic increase in the grants budget, the inflation percentage that had heretofore been allowed only in the agency's administrative budget.

● Growth in state programming dollars would receive legislative support if accomplished through carefully planned new programs or identification of specific organizations that needed assistance.

● Funding patterns had to demonstrate a balanced response to both artists and arts organizations, to supporting Native Alaskan arts resources as well as transplanted and visiting artists and arts companies, to a variety of styles within each arts discipline, and to a strengthening of those artforms that were particularly weak throughout the state or within a given geographic area.

● Grants programs were directed toward strengthening the economic system in which Alaska artists had to survive with an emphasis on development of new

63

Governor's budget request. This process enabled the Council to establish closer, more supportive relationships with key institutions. As a parallel strategy, the Council worked with smaller organizations to develop broad program initiatives.

The most difficult part of the Council's growth was the apparent necessity to accept line items in the programming budget. The Legislature was willing to support growth, but members sometimes wanted to mandate which organizations should get funding. Although the line items became additions to the budget and were not binding on the Council if the Governor exercised his line-item veto power, they caused problems in Council program evaluation. As more organizations sought line items, the legislators realized that they had assumed the functions of an administrative agency. A movement is currently underway to disallow line items but to fund the Council at a level sufficient to respond to varied needs.

With continued growth, the Alaska State Council on the Arts' fiscal year 1981 budget totals $1,930,700, or $4.76 per capita, easily the largest per capita funding of any state or territory.

approaches to support the arts, such as the percent-for-art program and the Alaskan Art Bank.

The Council's strategies were as follows:

• The Council convened a hearing panel that offered every arts organization an opportunity to make a presentation regarding its needs. Legislative support substantially increased after two House members, both from the Finance Committee, sat with Council members on that panel. Both legislators were convinced that state arts funding should be increased, and they became important allies in this struggle. On the Senate side, key contacts were members of the free conference committee, who, when the chips were down, were willing to watch over the arts budget and barter for increases. The Council's task was to make sure that key constituents and business associates supplied the committee members with necessary information.

• A network of community arts councils became the backbone of a statewide support system with the larger agencies coordinating with the smaller ones. An informal telephone and letter-writing network was so effectively established that, during bitter negotiations on proposed budget cuts, the Speaker of the Senate stated on the floor that he had received more letters from art lovers than from state employees who were seeking a substantial pay raise. At the same time he vowed that the arts would not be sacrificed.

• The Council worked closely with major developing organizations to reach advance agreement on funding. These funding levels were incorporated into a budget proposal submitted as an alternative to the

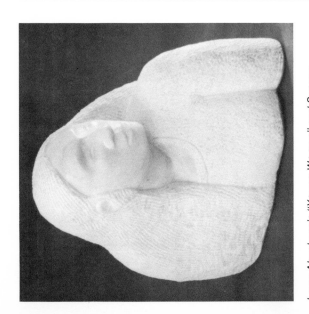

Larry Ahvakana's "Young Woman" and Spence Guerin's "Woman" are two of the more than 400 works purchased by the Alaskan Art Bank from 1975-1980. The Art Bank provides direct support to Alaskan artists and heightens awareness of contemporary arts.

CALIFORNIA

The California Arts Council's budget, which was only $1.4 million (7¢ per capita) for the 1978-1979 fiscal year following the June, 1978 passage of Proposition 13, rose dramatically by 500% to $7.3 million for 1979-1980 and increased again to $10.2 million for 1980-1981. The main factor in this growth was a unified advocacy campaign directed by the California Confederation of the Arts, a statewide, nonprofit, multidisciplinary arts service organization.

In the wake of Proposition 13's passage, an arts community that had been seriously fragmented unified behind the Confederation's leadership as an effective advocacy force. This sudden cohesion

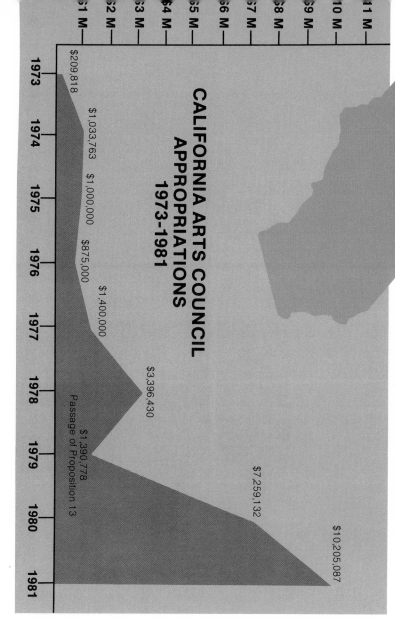

CALIFORNIA ARTS COUNCIL APPROPRIATIONS 1973-1981

$209,818 — 1973
$1,033,763 — 1974
$1,000,000 — 1975
$875,000 — 1976
$1,400,000 — 1977
$3,396,430 — 1978
$1,390,778 Passage of Proposition 13 — 1979
$7,259,132 — 1980
$10,205,087 — 1981

resulted from: (1) a greatly expanded arts budget proposal that, if approved, offered financial and technical assistance to many more artists and arts organizations; (2) the fact that the proposed budget was developed collectively by the Arts Council's members and staff and the Confederation's leaders and was agreed to by the Governor; (3) a recognition that an increased arts budget depended on active involvement in the legislative process; (4) a survival instinct that was awakened by Proposition 13's passage; and (5) a more favorable perception within the Legislature of the Arts Council's administrative capabilities.

To direct its advocacy campaign, the Confederation divided the state geographically and created seven regional advocacy committees. Each committee was chaired by a Confederation member or board director and was comprised of 30 to 50 artists, arts administrators, and interested individuals. Each committee organized subcommittees around the following tasks: (1) massive letter-writing campaigns to state legislators; (2) visits to every member of the Legislature in the region; (3) press relations and letters to the editor; (4) endorsements from non-arts organizations — for example, from the PTA, League of Women Voters, labor unions, chambers of commerce, community service and recreation organizations, and from local government officials; and (5) identification of people interested or involved in the arts who had been campaign contributors to key legislators and who would make appropriate contacts.

During the six-month period when the arts budget was before the Legislature, advocacy activities were conducted

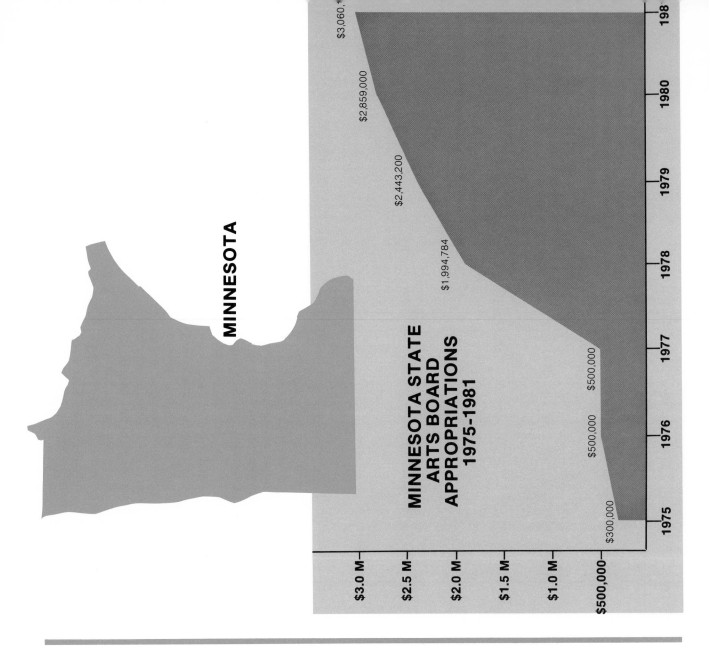

MINNESOTA

MINNESOTA STATE ARTS BOARD APPROPRIATIONS 1975-1981

$3,060,1

$2,859,000

$2,443,200

$1,994,784

$500,000

$500,000

$300,000

$3.0 M

$2.5 M

$2.0 M

$1.5 M

$1.0 M

$500,000

1975   1976   1977   1978   1979   1980   198

throughout the state. The Confederation's executive director communicated all budget-related legislative activity to the people chairing the regional committees who, in turn, related important information to committee members.

To augment the committees' activities, the Confederation sent monthly Advocacy Action Memos to its mailing list of 11,000 arts organizations and individuals throughout the state urging them to contact their own state senator and assembly member.

In addition, the Confederation sponsored an Arts Rally in Sacramento to demonstrate visibly the California arts community's support for the proposed budget. More than 400 arts representatives attended the rally and visited their legislators to urge passage of the arts budget and to explain a fact sheet describing the economic and social impact of arts programs in their districts.

Confederation board members made personal visits to key legislators, especially to members of the budget subcommittees and to the legislative leadership.

As the budget passed each critical step in the legislative process, the Confederation and its members sent thank-you letters and mailgrams to each member of the Legislature expressing appreciation on behalf of the statewide arts community.

This tremendous increase in California's arts budget from $1.4 million to $10.2 million in just two years demonstrated what can be accomplished when interested citizens become active, mobilize their talents, and carefully organize and orchestrate an advocacy campaign.

Citizens for the Arts/Minnesota Citizens for the Arts (CA/MCA) was created in November, 1975, to lobby for the Minnesota State Arts Board's biennial appropriation.

Citizens for the Arts is a membership, nonprofit, tax-exempt, statewide organization that provides a voice for artists, arts organizations, and arts consumers. Minnesota Citizens for the Arts is the political organization employing a professional lobbyist in the state capital and effective lobbying at the grassroots level.

During 1977 CA/MCA conducted a successful campaign to increase the state art board's biennial appropriation from $1 to $4 million. Then in 1979 the organization persuaded the Legislature to increase the biennial appropriation to $5.9 million, placing Minnesota eleventh among the states and special jurisdictions with 75¢ per capita in arts funding.

The following remarks by Carole Achterhof, past vice-president of Citizens for the Arts, and later a member of the Minnesota State Arts Board, first appeared in the May/June 1979 issue of *Museum News* and are reprinted with permission of the American Association of Museums.

"CA/MCA began its present 'key contact' system in the fall of 1976. One CA/MCA member in each legislative district was responsible for voicing the voters' concerns to his legislator. This network of members set up individual meetings with the 50 members of the House Appropriations and the Senate Finance committees in their home districts. Fifteen to 20 friends and neighbors of each legislator were invited to attend and discuss the needs of the arts in his own area. When it was impossible for legislators to meet in their hometowns, CA/MCA members met with them at their capitol offices.

"Each legislative committee member was educated on the proposed distribution plan, the needs of his constituents, and how they hoped he would vote on the upcoming appropriation for the arts. These CA/MCA members, in cooperation with the Minnesota State Arts Board, were able to assure their legislators that specific amounts would be spent for the arts in their own districts. Many of these legislator's, upon learning from their own constituents about these arts activities and what this amount of money would mean to their communities, immediately turned from anti-arts to pro-arts.

"CA/MCA also orchestrated the public testimony presented before the House Appropriations Semi-State Division. Three CA/MCA members came from outstate areas to describe what the additional monies would generate back home.

"CA/MCA met in planning sessions with leaders of both houses and discovered that five letters to a legislator on a single subject is a groundswell. One senator from the southwestern corner of the state voted against the arts increase in a subcommittee on the Thursday before Easter. After receiving hundreds of phone calls from constituents during the Easter weekend and a telegram with over 450 signatures on the following Monday morning, he learned how important the arts really were to his voters. He changed his vote to support an increase and has since become very friendly and supportive toward the arts. CA/MCA members were notified that the senator had changed his vote and appropriate letters of gratitude were sent to him.

"The $4 million appropriation eventually did pass in 1977, with unanimous votes in both house committees and on the Senate and House floors.

"CA/MCA's lobbying checklist includes the following points:

• Humanize your presentations to political committees. Be factual, but reach them where they live. Give examples of projects, successes, hopes and dreams of actual cases that affect their constituents. Emphasize people and people projects.

• Research and be aware of the committee members' concerns and interests. Direct any testimony or presentation to those interests. Select people to testify dependent on the makeup of the committee.

• Legislators come to their conclusions not as a result of endless facts and boring figures, but when they see the commitment and excitement in the people.

• Be totally appreciative toward your legislators. In January of this year, CA/MCA sponsored a Legislative Appreciation Event, where over 90 percent of the legislators and their guests were treated to a performance of the Minnesota Orchestra and exhibits from arts organizations, large and small, from all over the state."[1]

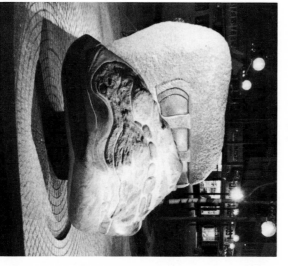

"*Granite Trio*" from the St. Cloud, Minnesota Art-in-Public-Places program.

NOTES
1. Copyright 1979 American Association of Museums.

New York ranks first among the states and territories in total arts funding. The New York State Council of the Arts' current budget of $33 million accounts for nearly one-third of total state arts funding for the 1980 fiscal year. At the Arts Task Force's May 1979, New York City meeting, Eric Larrabee, former Council Executive Director, discussed the New York experience with funding the arts. Following are excerpts from Mr. Larrabee's remarks.

"There are many ways in which the New York example is, if not unique, certainly possessing features that are duplicated only in degrees in other states. There is a remarkable combination of different factors that came together all at once which made the extraordinary increase in funding possible. And I'd like to mention some of them....

"The first is obviously that it is a state extremely rich in cultural resources, and was, long before the Council began. And also a state of extraordinary diversity, which contains not only this megalopolis we are in now, but a half dozen other substantial cities, and a very large rural population, third largest in the nation....

"Another factor was that in 1970 there really was a crisis. I know the word 'crisis' is very badly overused in our times, but I think one can genuinely say of the arts organizations of New York that in 1970 they were in deep, deep trouble....

"A third factor is the emergence of an organized, vocal, intelligent, energetic constituency. It was a combination of the potential availability of the money and of the genuine need that caused the constituency to mobilize itself. From 1970 on, beginning with the creation of a group called the Concerned Citizens for the Arts and with the gradual maturing of that group, we had in existence in this state a body of citizens prepared, willing, and able to make their desires and needs felt...."

NEW YORK

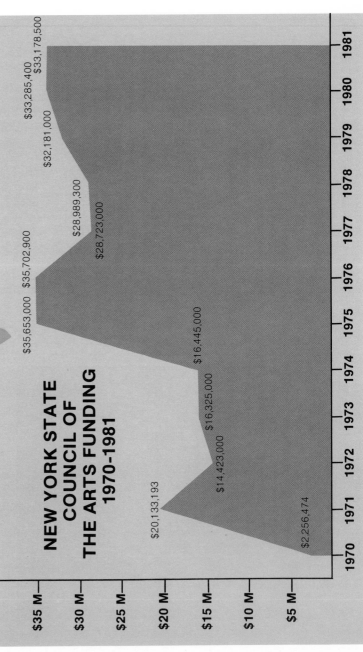

NEW YORK STATE COUNCIL OF THE ARTS FUNDING 1970-1981

$35,653,000 $35,702,900

$33,285,400
$33,178,500

$32,181,000

$28,989,300

$28,723,000

$20,133,193

$16,445,000

$16,325,000

$14,423,000

$2,256,474

$35 M
$30 M
$25 M
$20 M
$15 M
$10 M
$5 M

1970   1971   1972   1973   1974   1975   1976   1977   1978   1979   1980   1981

"Another element which has had a great effect is the existence of a Senate Special Committee which has looked into the Council's affairs from time to time....

"We have also increased the budget by, I have to confess, quite a lot of hard work on our own part. It's one of the necessary fictions of American life that government agencies do not lobby on their own behalf, but God help anyone that doesn't. It's a difference between what is technically illegal but permissible, and what is technically illegal and very definitely not permissible, and you have to discover how early on that somebody better be physically present in Albany every day the Legislature is in session.... You have to be literally in minute to minute touch with what is going on. And what this amounts to is largely a matter of information. Votes as you know are counted in quantity, but they have to be worked for one by one. And if somebody is unhappy about what the arts council is doing, you better know about it, you better know somebody talks to them and explains at least what you think you're doing and why the situation that has bothered them has come into existence."

New York State Senator Tarky Lombardi, Jr., Chairman of the State Senate Special Committee on the Culture Industry, adds another and perhaps most important factor.

"The very existence of the Council and its nurturing through the years was due to the vision and foresight of one man, Governor Nelson A. Rockefeller. In 1970, after a decade of existence, the Governor's vision of the Council took a quantum leap forward:

He proposed increasing its appropriation by nearly 1,000 per cent to $20 million, and the Legislature agreed. In making the recommendation, the Governor said:

'To consider our State without the arts, its museums and libraries, and its symphonies, operas and performing arts centers, is to imagine a cultural wasteland without pride or inspiration for our citizens.'

"The poet W. B. Yeats said the rhetorician would deceive his neighbor, the sentimentalist himself, but Governor Rockefeller in his dealings with the Council was neither a sentimentalist nor a rhetorician. He meant what he said. He truly saw the importance of money to the arts. For the first half-decade of the 70's the Council budget increased every year, reaching a high of $35 million."[5]

Legislative appropriations to the Utah Arts Council increased over 1,200% during the 1970's from $83,000 in 1970 to $1,175,600 a decade later. In fiscal 1980, per capita spending was 83.3¢, making Utah eighth in the nation. It is not by coincidence that a western state of less than moderate population is among the top ten in per-capita arts spending.

In 1899, the Utah Legislature created the first state arts agency, the Utah Art Institute, and endowed it with $2,000 for the biennium to advance the arts throughout the state. This early base of state legislative support became a major catalyst in creating a strong bond among public entities, local and community arts groups, major touring organizations and individual artists in all disciplines. In 1980, that bond is strengthened by continued support from the Executive and Legislative branches, guidance by the Department of Community and Economic Development, of which the Utah Arts Council is a division, and the recent establishment of both a statewide nonprofit arts advocacy organization, Utah Citizens for the Arts, and a statewide association of community arts agencies, the Utah Community Arts Agency Network (UCAAN).

Another factor contributing to continued growth of state arts support is ARTS-CAP (Community Action Planning for the Arts), one of the Utah Arts Council's community outreach programs. The program was designed to determine the needs of the arts community in Utah through a series of regional meetings and task forces. Two statewide Congresses growing out of ARTS-CAP developed a body of recommendations that will help to shape the future of the arts in Utah.

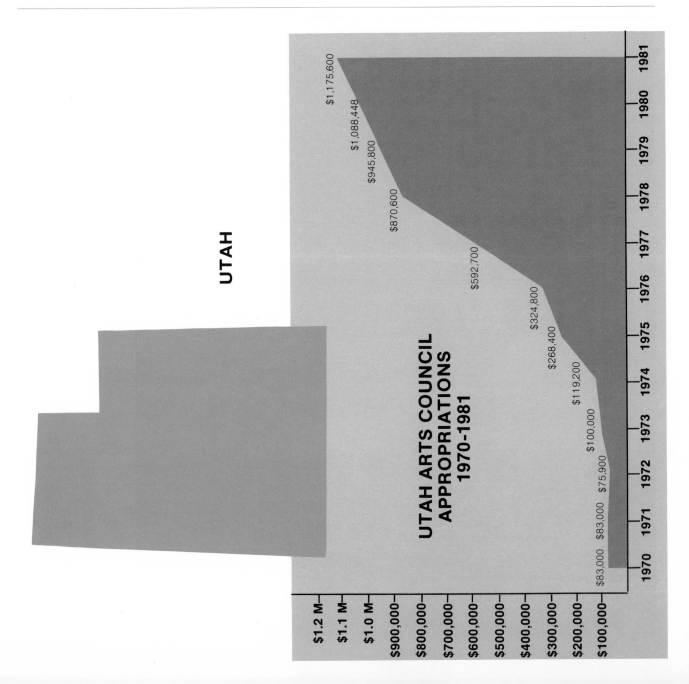

UTAH

UTAH ARTS COUNCIL APPROPRIATIONS 1970-1981

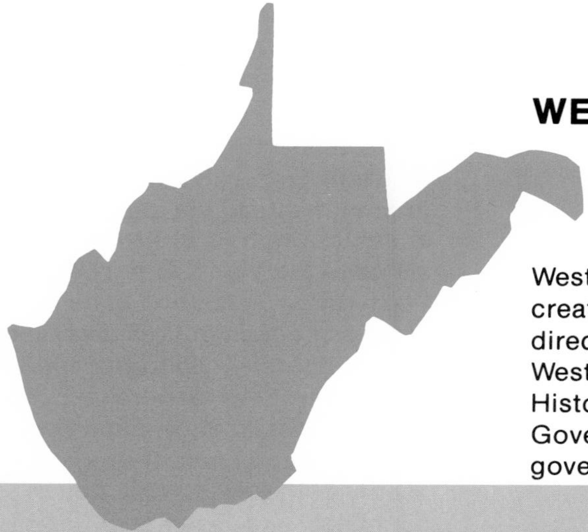

WEST VIRGINIA

WEST VIRGINIA ARTS FUNDING 1976-1981

$360,000

$360,000

$500,000

$1,320,300

$1,562,746

$1,636,327

$1.6 M

$1.4 M

$1.2 M

$1.0 M

00,000

00,000

00,000

00,000

$360,000

1976 1977 1978 1979 1980 1981

West Virginia is one of eight states that has created a department to administer and give direction to state cultural activities. The West Virginia Department of Culture and History was formed in 1977 as part of Governor John D. Rockefeller IV's government reorganization plan. The legislation brought together, under a department structure, agencies in the arts and humanities, archives and history, historic preservation, the state museum, arts and crafts, and the state's multi-purpose Cultural Center.

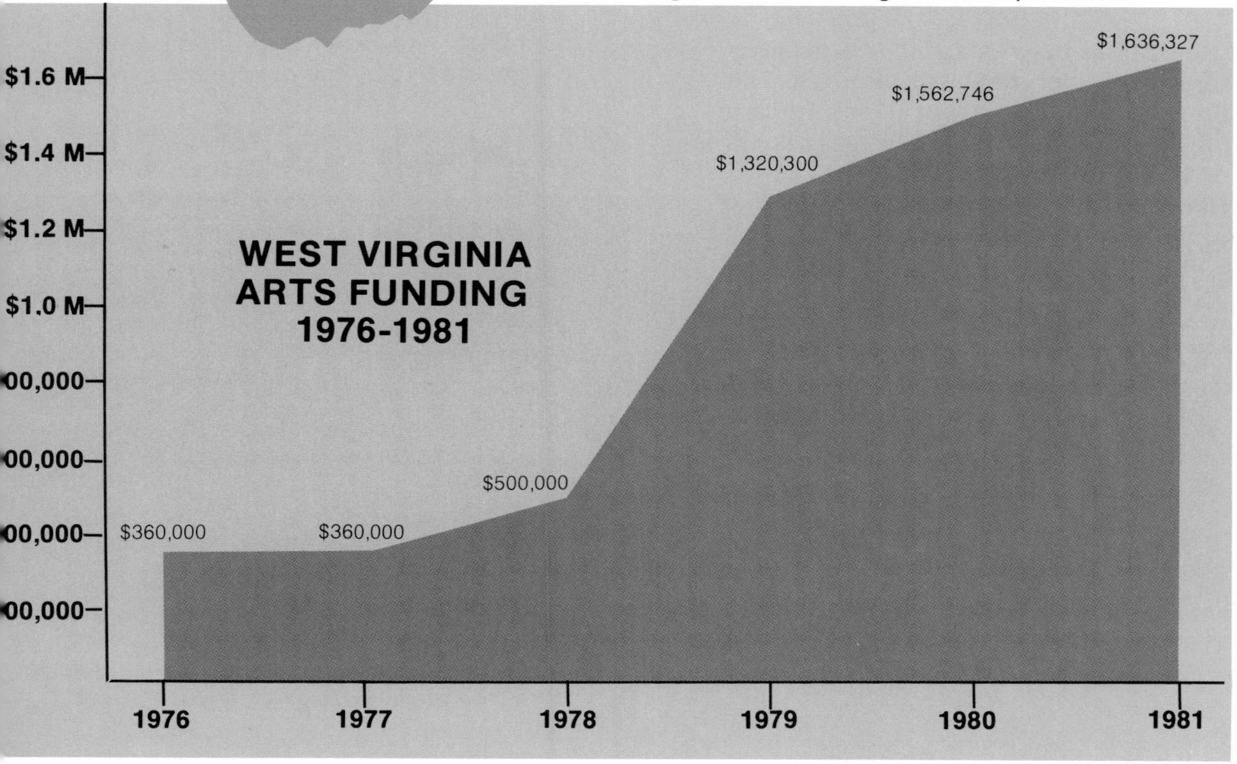

As an outgrowth of the Department's creation, the state's cultural funding has increased markedly. For example, the arts budget rose from $500,000 the year before the Department's commencement to the 1980-81 level of $1.6 million, ranking West Virginia fifth among all states in per-capita arts funding.

The key to the Department's success is the coordinating of services among the included agencies. Prior to the Department's creation, the components of the state's cultural support system had been working autonomously. Now the sharing of information and the cooperation among the Department divisions have created a new respect for state cultural support among both the public and members of the State Legislature. Cultural programming has become more visible and is reaching all areas of the state. One important feature is that the administrative costs and services, including personnel, of all department agencies are combined and presented as one portion of the Department's budget, rather than as part of each agency's budget.

Credit for the Department of Culture and History's success should be given to the last two governors' creative approach to state cultural activities, to an aware citizens' arts commission and its competent staff, and to a growing recognition by West Virginians of the importance of the arts and culture and the role of state government in fostering expansion of cultural opportunities.

Legislators who are committee and task force members are important arts advocates. Their colleagues often rely on their judgment on arts-related issues, including arts agency budget allocations.

Another way that legislators act as arts advisors and advocates is through legislative representation on or appointments to the state arts council or commission. By statute or policy, four states — Maryland, Ohio, Pennsylvania, and Washington — appoint state legislators to serve as council or commission members. In two others — California and Connecticut — the legislative leadership of each house appoints arts agency members. In Connecticut, in fact, the legislature appoints twenty of the twenty-five commission members — ten are appointed by each house and five by the governor.

Legislatures in at least fourteen states and Guam have established committees for consideration of arts issues. Hawaii, Louisiana, New York, North Carolina and Guam have standing committees on the arts and culture; arts subcommittees, joint committees, special or select committees, or legislative task forces have been created in thirteen other states.[1] The standing committees and subcommittees act on pending arts and culture legislation, while the other committees play an important advisory role, reviewing the proposed state arts agency budget, reporting on arts legislation and arts agency operations, or generally acting as a buffer between the legislature and the arts agency or arts community.

Other states have established arts task forces on which state legislators sit. The South Carolina Governor's Task Force on the Arts and the Massachusetts Task Force on Public Financing of the Arts and Humanities are examples.

"Since its inception Delegate Pauline Menes and I have served on the Maryland State Arts Council as designees of the President of the Senate and Speaker of the House, respectively. On balance, I think our being members has worked very well. Many legislators still consider the arts to be a frill, and the Arts Council budget is invariably scrutinized by the appropriations committees.

"As legislators serving on the Council, we have become familiar with policy, procedures, and programs and are the leading advocates for the arts in our respective chambers. A danger in having legislators serve on the Council is that we could lose objectivity — the old 'not-being-able-to-see-the-forest-for-the-trees' bit.

"Despite inherent dangers of legislative

"The South Carolina Governor's Task Force has further stimulated interest in the arts among the Governor and state officials and decision-makers. Our three subcommittees — education, business, and government — learn from each other and reinforce each other's activities in the arts."

—South Carolina Representative Harriet Keyserling

"Connecticut has had an ad hoc committee on the arts. The significant thing about the committee is that legislative leaders sit on it and it is therefore influential. We review the arts commission's budget before it is submitted and discuss with commission members and staff what is possible and what is not possible."

—Connecticut State Senator Lawrence J. DeNardis

"In Ohio the arts in effect have their own lobbyists in the four legislators who serve as non-voting members of the arts council."

—Ohio State Senator Stanley Aronoff

"The Legislature is rather proud of the Ohio Arts Council. That belief has been transmitted to a greater funding commitment at a time of retrenchment in state government spending."

— Ohio Representative Patrick A. Sweeney

members serving on executive boards, I believe an exception should be made in the area of the arts, at least until we have more enlightened thinking in this country."

—*Maryland State Senator Julian Lapides*

"I'm confident that Maryland has gained by my being a member of the Task Force. I bring back to our Maryland Arts Council many of the ideas that I have gained by the interchange with Task Force members from other states. I've learned what they are doing, what they've found successful, and what I think can be used in Maryland to our advantage."

— *Pauline Menes, Member, Maryland House of Delegates and Maryland Arts Council.*

The other approach of the legislature appointing non-legislators to the arts council may provide less direct legislative involvement, but does provide a vital link between the agency and the legislature.

"When it is budget time, the arts people don't go see the governor. They come to see us, the legislators. They put the load and the heat on us... One of the ways we can do more for the arts in our states is by becoming directly involved in making appointments."

—*New York Assemblyman William Passannante*

Legislators interested in the arts can aid arts council members and staff in another way, too:

"Take upon yourselves the role of holding the hand of the executive director of the council in your state, try to keep them from making political mistakes, and guide them through the political maze in your house and the other house and through the halls of the capitol. This can be of inestimable help."

—*William Passannante*

NOTE:
1. The chart on pages 10-11 indicates these states. New York has two committees — a standing Assembly committee and a special Senate committee.

BIBLIOGRAPHY

THE ECONOMIC IMPACT APPROACH

Baumol, William, *The Impact of the Broadway Theatre on the Economy of New York City: A Study for the League of New York Theatres and Producers, Inc.*, Princeton, New Jersey, Mathtech, Inc. (1977).

Blaug, Mark (Ed.), *The Economics of the Arts*, London, Martin Robertson and Company (1976).

Chicago Council on Fine Arts, *A Survey of Arts and Cultural Activities in Chicago* (1977).

Cwi, David, *The Role of the Arts in Urban Economic Development*, Washington, D.C., United States Department of Commerce (September 1980).

Cwi, David, and Lyall, Katherine, *The Economic Impact of Arts and Cultural Institutions*, Washington, D.C., National Endowment for the Arts (Report #6) (November 1977).

The Greater Philadelphia Cultural Alliance, *An Introduction to the Economics of Philadelphia's Cultural Organizations*, Philadelphia, The Pennsylvania Council on the Arts (1975).

Perloff, Harvey S., *The Arts in the Economic Life of the City*, New York, American Council for the Arts (1979).

Sullivan, John J., and Wassall, Gregory, *The Impact of the Arts on Connecticut's Economy*, Hartford, Connecticut, Connecticut Commission on the Arts (1977).

Washington Regional Arts Project, *The Arts in Metropolitan Washington*, Washington, D.C., Washington Center for Metropolitan Studies (1975).

Wolf, Thomas and Wassail, Gregory H., *The Arts and the New England Economy*, Cambridge, New England Foundation for the Arts (1980).

PUBLIC SUPPORT FOR THE ARTS

Harris, Louis, *Americans and the Arts*, New York, American Council for the Arts (1980).

Harris, Louis, *Americans and the Arts*, New York, American Council for the Arts (1975).

Netzer, Dick, *The Subsidized Muse — Public Support for the Arts in the United States*, Cambridge, Cambridge University Press (1978).

GOVERNMENT ARTS SUPPORT— AN HISTORICAL PERSPECTIVE

O'Connor, Francis V., *Federal Support for the Visual Arts: The New Deal and Now*, Greenwich, Connecticut, New York Graphic Society, Ltd. (1969).

Purcell, Ralph, *Government and Art*, Washington, D.C., Public Affairs Press (1956).

INNOVATIVE STATE ARTS LAWS AND PROGRAMS

Each state has created its own arts laws and programs. Many have enacted one or more of the Arts Task Force recommendations. These are summarized by the charts on pages 10 and 86.

In addition, each state has created exemplary or unique programs that are highlighted in the following state-by-state analysis. The programs presented in this section are not necessarily a state's most important or successful.

South Dakota Arts Council support has made possible public musical and theatrical performances by the Dakota Theatre Caravan. (See page 81.)

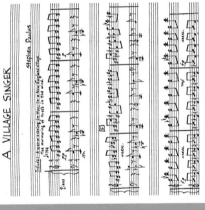

Missouri Arts Council funding of the Opera Theatre of St. Louis has drawn thousands of first-time patrons to operas such as "A Village Singer" by Stephen Paulus. (See page 78.)

"Early Spring" was created under Hawaii's percent-for-art legislation, the first statute of its kind enacted in the United States. (See page 76.)

ALABAMA

Alabama has one of the few state-supported schools of fine arts in the country. The high school provides training for talented young people considering careers in the arts.

Each year the Alabama Superintendent of Education conducts a statewide arts competition that awards prizes to elementary, junior high, and high school students.

The Alabama Festival of the Arts, held in Birmingham every spring, is each year dedicated to the arts of a different country.

ALASKA

The Alaskan Contemporary Art Bank is the best developed in the nation. Ninety-five percent of the more than 350 works that have been acquired under the program are currently on loan to state agencies. The works, all portable, are placed in public view, primarily in state leased buildings where the state's percent-for-art program is inapplicable.

Alaska's percent-for-art statute is unique in that it requires a minimum of one-half percent of the cost of constructing **rural** schools to be allocated for artworks.[1] (The state pays for construction of local schools.)

Recognizing that the piano is the basic instrument in most music programs, the Alaska State Council of the Arts' Piano Maintenance Program shares the cost of piano tuning with local communities.

ARIZONA

Arizona is the only state with a sales tax exemption covering direct sales by artists of their own artworks. The exemption does not apply when the artist sells through a gallery or other agent.[2]

The Arizona Commission on the Arts has established a Bi-Cultural Program with Mexico under which art exhibits and theatre groups from Mexico tour throughout Arizona and vice-versa.

The Commission has subsidized a Ticket Discount Program enabling disabled, elderly, and young persons to attend arts performances, exhibits, and events.

ARKANSAS

Arkansas presented its first annual Governor's Business and the Arts Awards in June 1980. Co-sponsored by the Arkansas Arts Council and the Department of Economic Development, the awards went to six Arkansas corporations for their exemplary arts support.

Apprentices in the Arts is a federally funded (Department of Labor/CETA) program administered by the Arkansas Arts Council that provides an artist with five apprentices to execute a public artwork for a community. Funded at $400,000 annually, the program trains disadvantaged youth for jobs associated with the construction and installation of public art, such as masonry, plumbing, electrical skills, and carpentry. The art is placed in schools, parks, along roadways, and in other public places.

CALIFORNIA

The California Arts Council's Maestro-Apprentice Program supports the preservation of artistic excellence and endangered crafts by funding acknowledged master California artists to engage an apprentice for one year.

The Arts Council has fostered a series of written agreements for joint sponsorship of arts programs with other state agencies, including the corrections, education, health, mental health, parks and recreation, and rehabilitation departments.

The California Jazz Award is given to a composer, musician, or vocalist who has made a significant contribution to jazz in the state. Benny Goodman was the first recipient of the award.

California is the only state thus far that has enacted statutes to provide visual artists a royalty on profitable resales of their work[3] and to protect artists against intentional alteration or destruction of their art.[4]

COLORADO

Colorado law exempts from property taxes business and other privately-owned art that is publicly displayed at least two weeks a year.[5]

The Colorado Council on the Arts and Humanities funds and administers the Chautauqua Touring Program, a traveling arts festival presenting theatre, dance groups, artists, and craftspeople who spend five days in each of a half-dozen rural communities during the summer. The program fulfills three purposes: It brings arts to rural areas, provides employment for artists, and trains small communities in sponsoring arts events.

Colorado has undertaken a State Design Program intended to improve the graphic design of state government stationery and forms.

CONNECTICUT

In 1980 Connecticut enacted legislation requiring each community cable television operator to "maintain at least one specially designated, non-commercial, public access channel available on a first-come, nondiscriminatory basis."[6] The new law is in response to a recent United States Supreme Court decision that left to the states the issue of mandating community access cable television channels.[7]

During 1980 the Connecticut Commission on the Arts refused to accept a $100,000 appropriation from the Legislature because it was conditioned on the Commission raising $50,000 in private contributions. The Commission reasoned that it would be competing with its grants recipients who were also trying to raise private funds, that it was inappropriate for a taxpayer-supported, state grants-making agency to solicit private funds, that any such solicitation would establish an undesirable precedent for other government agencies, and that it might be lobbied by private contributors to make grants to particular individuals or organizations.

DELAWARE

The Delaware State Arts Council's Mini Grants Program makes one-time grants of $500 or less available to the state's arts organizations for emergency needs that could not have been foreseen.

The Council's Ticket Sharing Program subsidizes tickets for young people to attend arts events. The program is most often used by schools, with the arts agency paying 60% of the ticket cost and the school 40%.

FLORIDA

In 1978 the House of Representatives appropriated $75,000 for an art acquisition program to enhance public spaces in the new House facilities. More than five-hundred Florida artists submitted slides from which the House purchased 79 panel-recommended artworks by 52 Florida artists. In 1980 the House appropriated an additional $50,000 for a sculpture acquisition program.

"The House of Representatives art acquisition program is an exemplary effort by a state to support its artists by purchase and recognition."
—Florida Representative Joseph Gersten

On his official stationery, Secretary of State George Firestone describes Florida as the "State of the Arts."

Florida law authorizes local government to use proceeds from dog and horse races to fund cultural activities.[8]

The Fine Arts Council will soon begin the Florida Orchestra Outreach Program to support regional symphony orchestras. The orchestras will make one-day tours to cities of under 10,000, visiting schools during the day and presenting community performances in the evening.

GEORGIA

The State Senate 1979 Interim Committee on the Arts and Tourism recommended (1) to use the arts as an economic development and redevelopment tool and to promote tourism and artist employment, (2) to foster interdepartmental cooperation among state cultural, economic development, and tourism agencies, and (3) to deliver arts services to special populations through education and audience development.

The Council for the Arts and Humanities sponsors the Georgia Art Bus, a program that sends two education exhibits, "Contemporary Crafts" and "Patterns," for three-week periods to schools, primarily in rural areas. Artists in residence offer additional instruction and information. One bus also transports an exhibit titled "Georgia Artists: State Collection" for display in public and private facilities. Georgia spends about $10,000 each year to add new works to the state collection.

The Council's Crafts Program is conducting surveys of different regions to determine marketing and educational opportunities for the state's craftspeople. The Council produces publications listing Georgians involved with crafts. The publications are distributed to crafts fairs and festivals nationwide. The program also offers technical assistance in marketing and business practices.

GUAM

The Guam Legislature is one of the few with a standing committee that considers cultural issues—the Committee on Municipal and Cultural Affairs.

Legislation introduced in 1980 to create the Department of Cultural Affairs would have encompassed a variety of arts and cultural institutions and would have created a number of new programs, including an art bank.

HAWAII

Hawaii is one of only four states with a standing legislative committee on the arts — the House Committee on Culture and the Arts.

In 1967 Hawaii became the first state to enact a percent-for-art program.[9] The program displays purchased artwork in both state and county buildings. Another unusual feature of Hawaii's program is that it authorizes the purchase of student artwork, which is exhibited in schools throughout the state.

The Ethnic Heritage and Humanities Program receives substantial funding each year. Its purposes are to recognize and perpetuate the cultural heritage of the state's many ethnic groups.

IDAHO

The Idaho Commission on the Arts funds Immediate Assistance Grants. Arts organizations may apply for and immediately receive up to $500 for emergency situations, including unexpected performance and exhibit opportunities and sudden funding cut-offs. The Commission staff makes grant decisions consistent with Commission guidelines with after-the-fact Commission review. The program is funded at $14,000 for the 1980-81 fiscal year.

ILLINOIS

The Illinois Arts Council funds both purchase grants and project completion grants to Illinois creative artists. The purchase grants provide funding to museums, galleries, and other nonprofit organizations to buy artworks from state artists. The project completion grants allocate a maximum of $800 to allow an artist to complete a specific, partially finished effort. About 75% of the 455 applications submitted during fiscal 1980 were funded.

Each year the Council administers the Illinois Arts Week, a statewide celebration of the arts. The Council assists local communities with program ideas and coordinates poster design, printing, and distribution, news media coverage, and the Governor's Awards Program.

In order to establish, maintain, and operate cultural centers, Illinois law authorizes municipalities to issue bonds and, with voter approval, to impose a maximum .25% property tax.[10]

INDIANA

The Indiana Arts Commission annually monitors its grants to ensure that each of the state's 92 counties is served through Commission funding. In counties not receiving funding, the staff works with arts organizations to generate quality grant proposals. Legislators have been impressed with the Commission's diligence in dispersing funds statewide.

The Indiana Arts Awards are offered biennially to state artists who have made significant contributions to the arts nationally or internationally. The awards are presented by the governor and legislative leaders in ceremonies at the State House.

IOWA

Touring Arts Team, which was initiated in 1977, is a unique Iowa Arts Council program that sends professional artists into rural communities of fewer than 1,500. The team visits each town for 2½ days, leading classes and workshops, giving performances, and offering special projects to a broad cross-section of the community.

Arts in County Care Facilities, begun in 1977 with $10,000 in state funds, provides facilities with classes featuring a variety of artforms.

Faces of Iowa is a photographic exhibition of work by students in grades six through twelve. The exhibition appears each August at the Iowa State Fair and then tours the state for 12 months under the Council's touring exhibit program.

KANSAS

In 1979 Kansas became the first state to enact legislation restoring to artists a fair market value state income tax deduction for donations of their art to nonprofit galleries and museums.[11] The law previously had limited the artist's tax deduction to the cost of materials and supplies used.

Among the predominantly rural states, Kansas has perhaps the best developed community arts program. The Kansas Arts Commission encouraged development of and established funding for the Association of Community Arts Councils of Kansas. The Association provides the state's community arts agencies with technical assistance, a newsletter, and an annual statewide conference. As a result, Kansas' rural arts agencies, whether staffed by paid or volunteer personnel, operate in a businesslike and creative manner, utilizing and developing community resources. Many local agencies are implementing five-year community cultural plans.

"Kansas boasts a community arts program second to none. From ballet to baroque to bluegrass, Kansans are exposed to the arts through a variety of media and modes."
— Kansas Senator Ronald R. Hein

KENTUCKY

The Governor's Challenge Grants Program, administered by the Kentucky Arts Commission, provides state matches of up to one-third of an arts organization's total annual contributed income. Open to all Kentucky organizations that present or sponsor public arts events on a regular basis, the grants offer basic operating support and have successfully stimulated private funding for arts organizations. Program funding for fiscal 1981 is $704,000, increasing in fiscal 1982 to $1,126,200.

The Kentucky Legislature has appropriated $23.5 million to construct the Kentucky Center for the Arts in Louisville. The Legislature has also authorized the local county to impose an additional 1% hotel tax for center operating expenses.[12]

The Commission is preparing a statewide minority arts resource directory that will focus on Black artists and arts organizations. The directory will be based on a recently conducted survey.

Each year the Commission's Rural Libraries Program places poets in residence in rural libraries for five nine-week residencies. The poets offer readings and conduct workshops to stimulate interest in literature and to work with community writers who would not otherwise have an opportunity to work with a professional.

LOUISIANA

Each year the Louisiana State Arts Council's Awards Program honors one or more legislators who have been most active in supporting the arts.

The Business Council of 100 is comprised of business people from throughout the state who are interested in the arts. Appointed by the governor, the body advises the governor and appropriate state agencies regarding state arts policy and planning.

The Art-in-State-Buildings Program places representative works by recognized Louisiana artists in public areas of state buildings in the capitol complex.

MAINE

In 1979 Maine became the first state to authorize heirs to pay inheritance taxes with acceptable art.[13] Taxes arising from Maine artist Bernard Langley's estate were paid with art, and other estates are under consideration.

The Maine Commission on the Arts and Humanities administers rotating visual arts exhibits in the State House. Early in 1981, the Commission will expand the program to include performing arts.

The first Maine Cultural Heritage Week, statutorily created, was held in March, 1980.[14] The celebration featured visual and performing arts events showcasing the state's cultural resources.

MARYLAND

Nonprofit organizations receiving grants from the State Arts Council and presenting an annual series of scheduled cultural events are exempt from amusement and admissions taxes.[15]

Distinctive Maryland State Arts Council programs include: (1) funding of a state study of artists' needs, for which a diversified 30-member panel has been created: (2) matching grants to small museums for acquisition and conservation projects; (3) preparation of an exhibition and catalogue of traditional Maryland folk arts; (4) Council-sponsored statewide vocal auditions; and (5) a slide catalogue of artists' works that artists may update annually.

MASSACHUSETTS

Massachusetts in 1979 enacted the first law establishing a state lottery to fund the arts.[16] The arts lottery is expected to generate $3 to $12 million annually through the sale of $5 tickets. Beginning in July, 1981, local arts councils will distribute revenues on a per-capita basis. More than 300 such councils have recently sprung up in anticipation of the funding. However, within the Massachusetts arts community concern exists that the $5 ticket price is too expensive to be popular, that the local agencies have been created without proper planning and may close down if the lottery is unsuccessful, that the lottery revenue will replace rather than supplement the Massachusetts Council on the Arts and Humanities' current funding, and that even if tickets sell, the lottery's expenses will leave little for arts programs.

The Metropolitan District Commission, which administers recreation programs in 78 cities and towns in the greater Boston area, has a percent-for-art program created by regulation. Under the program, art will enhance skating rinks, swimming pools, and other future outdoor recreation facilities. The Massachusetts Council, through its artists' foundation, will recommend works for commission or purchase.

MICHIGAN

The Michigan Artrain is unique — a train containing art exhibits and traveling statewide, with particular emphasis on servicing remote regions. The Artrain has extended its services to other states, providing a regional model for visual arts touring.

Michigan has been a leader in arts education. Among the state's actions and policies are:

• A legislatively created Arts in Education Advisory Council that helps to formulate State Department of Education policies on the arts;

• Seminars conducted by the state education department that instruct teachers on integrating the arts into all modes of education;

• Very Special Arts Festivals that integrate the arts into special education by involving disabled children in arts experiences and developing arts skills; and

• A State Board of Education policy statement calling for comprehensive arts planning in all educational institutions.

MINNESOTA

A 1980 law exempts arts events from state sales taxes and repeals the authority of local government in Minneapolis and St. Paul to impose an entertainment tax.[17]

The Minnesota State Arts Board's unique Regional Arts Council Program has established eleven regional councils whose jurisdiction corresponds to the state's economic development regions.

Minnesota Citizens for the Arts, the state's arts lobbying organization, sponsors an annual Legislative Night, providing state legislators and constitutional officers a chance to view the works of artists and arts organizations from around the state. More than half the legislators attend this annual event.

MISSISSIPPI

Pathways to Music is a pilot program funded by the Mississippi Arts Commission, the participating school district, and a private company in the music business. It enables kindergarten through fourth grade children to participate in creative music activities.

The Craftsmen's Guild of Mississippi was formed through a cooperative program of the Arts Commission and the Mississippi Agricultural and Industrial Board. The Guild operates a crafts shop, office and workshop space, and a School of Crafts and Design. Two statewide crafts festivals are held annually.

In 1979 Jackson, Mississippi hosted the first International Ballet Competition held in the United States.

MISSOURI

In 1979 the Missouri Arts Council sponsored a playwriting competition. All six plays written by the three winners and three runners-up were produced, and the competition led to creation of a statewide network of Missouri playwrights.

Opera Theatre of Saint Louis is a relatively new and overwhelmingly successful company. The Theatre, which receives $60,000 of its nearly $1 million budget from the Missouri Arts Council, concentrates on broadening opera's public appeal and has succeeded in attracting thousands of first-time opera-goers to its performances. In 1979 the company performed the world premiere of "A Village Singer," an Arts Council-commissioned opera.

MONTANA

Montana imposes a 30% tax on the value of coal extracted within the state. One-half of this tax revenue is directed by statute to the purchase of parks, restoration of artwork in the State Capitol, and other cultural purposes.[18] The Montana Arts Council has funded its folklorist program from coal tax revenue, and hopes to use this source to fund future cultural programs.

The Arts Council is producing arts programming for commercial television. (There is presently no public television station in Montana.) The initial productions featured ten half-hour interviews with Montana artists emphasizing the importance of the arts.

The Council's Community Arts Bookshelf

program has placed 450 arts reference books in 19 community and regional libraries statewide.

Artists Search is a computerized artists' registry maintained by the Council. The system presently provides interested artists with computer telegrams containing time-precious information about events. Artist-to-artist informational and educational communications and a registry of arts organizations will eventually be incorporated into the network.

NEBRASKA

The Nebraska Visitors' Development Act imposes a 1% state sales tax on hotel accommodations, the proceeds of which are used to promote state tourism, arts, and culture. The act also authorizes counties to impose an additional 2% hotel tax for local tourism, arts, and culture.[19]

The Nebraska Arts Council's economic impact study of the state's nonprofit arts organizations has been useful to the state agency in seeking increased appropriations.

The Council has a program of cooperation with the state's educational television network to fund locally produced arts programming.

Nebraska is one of the states receiving funds under the NEA's new jazz artist-in-schools residency program, through which jazz musicians perform and lead training workshops in schools.

NEVADA

The Governor's Commission on the Future of Nevada has included an arts and culture component in its report.

The Sierra Arts Foundation, funded in part by the Nevada Arts Council on the Arts, has published a handbook for arts organizations regarding federal regulations under Section 504 of the Rehabilitation Act of 1973. The handbook's principal purpose is to train staff to fulfill the needs of special constituencies.

NEW HAMPSHIRE

The New Hampshire Commission on the Arts' Poster Design Program offers $500 grants to New Hampshire artists to create a poster design promoting the activities of one of the state's arts organizations.

New Hampshire's percent-for-art statute uniquely supports purchase of both new art and art of historical significance.[20] This feature was helpful in securing legislative passage.

NEW JERSEY

The New Jersey State Council on the Arts each summer sponsors an Artist-Teacher Institute for classroom teachers and nationally and regionally known artists.

For the last four years, the Council has sponsored a statewide Summer Festival that features arts events in local parks, concert halls, and school auditoriums, as well as free performances, arts and crafts festivals, and a campsite artist-in-residence program at 24 state parks.

NEW MEXICO

The New Mexico Arts Division's Challenge Grants Program, which offers matching grants to community arts agencies, has greatly stimulated local arts funding and support in many New Mexico communities. In many instances, the local match has greatly exceeded the one-to-one state agency requirement.

A unique feature of the Arts Division's Artists-in-Schools Program is the extensive utilization of indigenous Native American, Hispanic, and Anglo folk artists for short-term school residencies.

NEW YORK

In 1980 the New York State Council on the Arts (NYSCA) marks its twentieth anniversary as the nation's leading state arts funding mechanism, currently granting more than $31 million to New York's arts and cultural organizations. The key to the Council's approach to its cultural support activities lies in two important legislative mandates to which it must adhere.

First, one-half of the Council's annual budget must go to "primary institutions." Second, NYSCA must fund arts services to the state's 62 counties on the basis of 55¢ per-capita of county population. These mandates are not mutually exclusive, for grants to primary institutions may be counted as fulfilling the per-capita requirement. Taken together, the mandates not only provide sustained support for the primary arts institutions, but also furnish a base of support for developing arts activities at the county and local level.

NORTH CAROLINA

Created in 1971, North Carolina's Department of Cultural Resources was the first cabinet-level department devoted exclusively to culture and the arts. The Department's three main divisions — archives and history, the arts, and the state library — annually administer appropriations exceeding $16 million.

The Visiting Artists Program is a Department of Community Colleges' administered project that places 50 artists in communities for nine- or ten-month residencies.

Grassroots Arts is a North Carolina Arts Council program that allocates money to counties based on their population (currently 10 cents per person). Created by statute,[21] the grants reach all 100 North Carolina counties and are matched at the local level. In each county, the community arts council determines recipients and administers distribution of the funds.

The North Carolina Symphony is the only major state-administered symphony in the nation. Forty-seven percent of the Symphony's $2.6 million annual budget is state funded. The Symphony's principal mission is to give free concerts to approximately 250,000 public school children. The Symphony also performs 120 evening concerts attended by more than 80,000 people.

NORTH DAKOTA

The state's two-year old Cultural Endowment Fund was established with $70,000 in state funds invested in interest-bearing securities and accounts. The North Dakota Council on the Arts is authorized to spend the interest earned by the Endowment on arts-related activities. The Fund also is authorized to accept private gifts.[22]

State law authorizes local jurisdictions to increase revenues ½% to fund local arts activities. The arts levy requires voter approval in municipalities of 2,500 or more.[23]

OHIO

The Ohio Arts Council is considering an arts stamps program that would offer families eligible for food stamps reduced rate tickets to arts events. The stamps would be redeemed by the Arts Council from participating arts institutions and organizations. This program is still in the development stages.

The Council's Minority Arts Development Program funds arts organizations which are Appalachian, Black, Hispanic, Native American Indian, and Oriental/Asian. A Minority Arts Task Force provides technical assistance to minority organizations to strengthen their operations and to assist them in the grants making process.

A 1979 state law authorizes local governments to form regional arts and cultural districts to be funded by voter-approved property tax increases. The districts would use the tax revenues to fund arts and cultural organizations within their territories.[24]

OKLAHOMA

Under Oklahoma's Capitol Arts Project, artists lend their works for placement in State Capitol legislative offices. The artists meet with legislators to present and discuss the works to be displayed. The program also features a series of noontime concerts at the Capitol.

"The Capitol Arts Project does not cost a lot of money, but builds goodwill that converts many legislators to supporters of the arts."
—Oklahoma Representative Hannah D. Atkins

The Oklahoma Summer Arts Institute, funded in part by the State Arts Council and held at a state-owned resort, is a summer program for talented high school youngsters. Scholarships are awarded to students unable to pay tuition.

OREGON

The Oregon Arts Commission operates a program of direct mail marketing of fine art prints created by northwest artists. Fifty-five prints have been selected through open competition. The works have been reproduced on large posters that are being distributed nationwide to individuals and businesses interested in purchasing and exhibiting prints, and the posters have also been exhibited in other states. About $12,000 worth of sales resulted from the first series of 35 prints, and 86% of the participating artists received exhibition offers. The program is an attempt by the Commission to use the free marketplace to further artists' careers.

The Arts Commission and the Department of Education jointly administer a program of Young Writers Fellowships awarded to high school juniors and seniors. The annual prize for the twelve winners is the chance to spend a week with nationally recognized writers who teach the students writing techniques.

PENNSYLVANIA

In 1979, the Pennsylvania Council on the Arts organized a special committee composed of private citizens, artists, and legislators who held public hearings statewide to gain insight into the problems and concerns of artists and arts organizations.

Expressions '80 was a June, 1980, minorities' arts festival in Philadelphia that attracted artists from a six-state area. It was the first regional festival of its kind in the Northeast.

The Legislative School Art Exhibit, started three years ago, is open to all Commonwealth elementary and secondary students. Opening ceremonies are held annually in the State Capitol Building, after which the art is displayed for a month.

PUERTO RICO

Puerto Rico has been a consistent leader in supporting the arts, having allocated nearly $50 million in arts funding over the past 15 years.

In 1980, legislation was enacted to create the cabinet-level Administration for the Development of the Arts and Culture.[25]

RHODE ISLAND

The Rhode Island State Council on the Arts' "Outdoor Gallery" billboard reproduces works by Rhode Island's professional artists and talented secondary school students. Each year the billboard is unveiled by the Governor in front of the Statehouse and then is toured throughout the state.

The Council has established an on-going relationship with the Rhode Island Lawyer Referral Service to aid artists with their legal problems.

SOUTH CAROLINA

The South Carolina Arts Commission's Architects in the Schools Program places professional architects in schools and communities for short and long-term residencies.

The Commission's Teacher Incentive Project offers teachers financial assistance to undertake innovative arts-related projects with their students.

The Commission-sponsored program, "Art of the Short Film Festival," makes available six 90-minute programs of independent films from around the world.

Stage South, South Carolina's State Theatre, tours statewide and regionally on a current annual budget of $125,000.

SOUTH DAKOTA

South Dakota is one of several states that makes unlawful the sale of products represented as authentic Native American arts and crafts unless such products are in fact authentic.[26]

South Dakota has been a leader in enacting historic and cultural preservation legislation. The state has established a state register of historic structures and sites[27] and a law providing a five-year moratorium on property tax increases resulting from rehabilitation of historic structures.[28]

TENNESSEE

Since 1972 the Tennessee Arts Commission has been working with craftspeople in rural and outlying areas and operating crafts shops in state parks. A 1980 state law requires that at least 25% of the crafts sold in state parks be native to the state.[29] The Arts Commission annually publishes a listing of arts and crafts festivals and fairs located throughout the Southeast. This publication is distributed to Tennessee artists and craftspeople as an aid in marketing their work. The Joe L. Evins Appalachian Center for Crafts, administered by Tennessee Tech University, is an outstanding new regional crafts school that began its first full-time student program in September 1980.

The Commission operates a joint arts-humanities program with the Tennessee Committee for the Humanities. With funds totalling $26,000 for fiscal 1980, the program sponsored several projects, each involving both scholars in the humanities and practicing artists.

TEXAS

Texas' state authorized hotel-motel occupancy tax has greatly stimulated local arts funding. If a locality imposes the full 4% tax permitted by state law, at least 1% must be allocated for arts or cultural activities, tourism, or historic preservation.[30]

The Texas Commission on the Arts has formed a Business Involvement Committee, comprised of three arts commissioners and seven businesspeople who coordinate activities to encourage business arts support. The Committee's 1979 survey of the state's arts organizations determined that nearly 8,000 Texas businesses had contributed to the arts that year. Each received a certificate of commendation for its support.

UTAH

Utah has a state art collection of more than 600 works in all media. Begun in 1899, the collection is made available for loan to state government offices, legislative members, and art galleries, and for tours throughout the state. Through a jurying process additional works by the state's artists are purchased annually.

Utah's arts agency enabling statute is unique in requiring professional artist representation on the state's arts council. The law specifies one representative from each of eight different arts disciplines on the thirteen-member body.[31]

The Utah Arts Festival, partially state funded, is an annual celebration of the arts in downtown Salt Lake City.

State-sponsored arts contests have a long tradition in Utah and were funded at $52,000 for the 1980 fiscal year. The Utah Arts Council aids winners among Utah's writers, playwrights, and visual artists in gaining publication, production, or exhibition of their entries.

VERMONT

The Vermont Council on the Arts has funded a pilot program of Radio Production Grants. Fifteen minute tapes designed to promote the arts will be distributed to commercial radio stations statewide. The theme of the first tapes is how Vermont has inspired artists in their work.

The Arts Loan Fund is part of Vermont's Job Start Program, administered by the State Office of Economic Opportunity. The Program offers visual, performing, and literary artists and arts organizations one year loans of $300-$600 at 5% interest for purchase of supplies, equipment, or other materials needed for marketing or display of their artforms.

VIRGINIA

The Virginia Museum of Fine Arts, a state agency, will receive more than $8 million in state funds for its 1981 and 1982 programs. The Richmond-based museum's 32 nonprofit local chapters act as local sponsors of museum exhibits, films, lecture series, resident artists, and an artmobile program.

The Virginia Opera Theatre brings touring professional opera productions into schools and communities statewide. Funded one-half by the state and one-half by local match, the Opera Theatre offers performances and vocal and technical workshops in 35 communities each year, reaching more than 50,000 people.

"The Virginia Opera Theatre is a model program ensuring that all people, young and old, rich and poor, can enjoy professional opera in English in their own community."

— Virginia Delegate Edythe C. Harrison

WASHINGTON

The Washington State ARTSPLAN is probably the most comprehensive state arts planning document to date. ARTSPLAN makes specific recommendations for state arts legislation and programs, provides a statewide directory of many arts facilities and organizations, and presents an economic impact study of the arts in Washington. It is the product of the Arts Alliance of Washington State, a volunteer citizens advocacy group representing the state's arts organizations.

The acquisition of artwork for the State Legislative Building is now in progress. In the first phase of a ten-year project, each of the chambers will receive $95,000 in art through a program administered by the Joint Legislative Arts Committee. The Committee also is empowered to solicit private funds to acquire art for the remainder of the building.

Among notable state laws affecting the arts are one statute allowing free use of school facilities for local cultural activities[32] and another allocating a portion of admissions to state college and university arts performances for performing arts scholarships.[33]

WEST VIRGINIA

West Virginia's Arts and Humanities Division operates several programs to aid the state's performing, visual, and literary artists in producing and presenting new works. Among the programs are:

- "Competitive Programs for Performing Artists," assists arts organizations in presenting new works by composers, playwrights, writers, poets, choreographers, and filmmakers.

- "Presenting West Virginia Artists" assists art institutions to present one person exhibits.

- The Division's "Buyers Market" brings together West Virginia visual artists and potential purchasers of their works.

- "The West Virginia Juried Exhibition" offers about $33,000 annually in purchase and merit awards to West Virginia artists.

WISCONSIN

The Wisconsin Arts Board's highly visible Barn Mural Program (illustrated at right) provided $80,000 to visual artists to paint decorative murals on barns statewide.

The Board's Wisconsin Project for Artists was a CETA-funded program that placed 50 artists on the Board's staff. The project had four components:

- Fifteen performing artists developed programs that toured state parks and rural festivals during two summers;

- Ten writers and photographers produced Wisconsin Images, a book containing poetry, short stories, and photography that is currently being distributed by the Arts Board;

- Twelve visual artists produced public artworks in local communities; and

- Thirteen artists comprised a management team that coordinated the program and produced publicity materials.

WYOMING

The Wyoming Council on the Arts funds the University of Wyoming Cultural Outreach Program that sends university arts resources throughout the state.

A Council-funded photographic documentary on mineral extraction, a controversial state issue, was first exhibited in the State Capitol and then toured statewide.

The Council also awards planning grants for arts facility restoration and construction and seeks private funding for folk arts residencies.

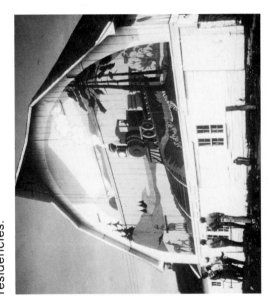

NOTES
1. Alaska Statutes, Section 35.27.020.
2. Tax Regulations of Arizona, Sales and Use Tax Division, Chapter 5, Regulation 15-5-1837.
3. California Civil Code, Section 986.
4. California Civil Code, Section 987.
5. Colorado Revised Statutes, Section 39-1-104.
6. Connecticut General Statutes, Section 16-333 (c).
7. The Federal Communications Commission v. Midwest Video, 440 U.S. 689 (1979).
8. Florida Statutes, Chapter 550.03.
9. Hawaii Revised Statutes, Section 103-8.
10. Illinois Statutes, Chapter 24, Section 11-45.1-1 and following.
11. Kansas Statutes, Chapter 79-32,120.
12. Kentucky Revised Statutes, Sections 153.410-153.450.
13. Maine Revised Statutes, Title 27, Sections 91-93, and Title 36, Section 3688.
14. Maine Revised Statutes, Title 1, Section 118.
15. Maryland Codes, Article 81, Section 406.
16. Massachusetts Laws, Chapter 10, Section 35A.
17. Minnesota Statutes, Section 297A.25(y).
18. Montana Revised Codes, Chapter 15, Section 84-1319(2)(h).
19. Revised Statutes of Nebraska, Sections 81-1253, 81-1254.
20. New Hampshire Revised Statutes, Title 19-A, Section 8.
21. North Carolina General Statutes, Section 143B-122.
22. North Dakota Century Code, Sections 54-54-08.1 and 08.2.
23. House Bill 1263, 1981 Session.
24. Ohio Revised Code, Section 3381.01 and following.
25. Puerto Rico Senate Bills 1154-1158, 1980 Session.
26. South Dakota Statutes, Chapter 37-7, Sections 1-3.
27. South Dakota Statutes, Chapter 1-19A.
28. South Dakota Statutes, Chapter 1-19A, Section 20.
29. Tennessee Code, Section 11-313.
30. Texas Civil Statutes, Article 1269j-4.1.
31. Utah Code, Section 65-2-4.
32. Revised Code of Washington, Chapter 28A.58.247.
33. Revised Code of Washington, Chapter 28B.10.704.

At its nine meetings, the Arts Task Force considered many areas of state arts involvement for which the group did not develop specific recommendations.

This section presents these important issues and offers suggestions for state action.

Basket-maker Dwight Stump, part of an Ohio Folk Artists-in-Schools program, demonstrates his craft. (See Folk Arts and Folklife Programs, page 89.)

The Dance Theatre of Harlem performs "The Four Temperaments". (See Minorities and the Arts, page 91.)

The Oregon Mime Theatre brings its high-quality professional artists into rural communities. (See Rural Areas and the Arts, page 88.)

STATE ARTS AGENCIES

Although the state arts agency in not exclusively a twentieth-century phenomenon — Utah created the first one in 1899 — as late as 1965, when Congress created the National Endowment for the Arts, only 18 agencies had been established. However, with the incentive of federal arts funding, by the end of 1967, all fifty states, as well as the District of Columbia, Puerto Rico, and the Virgin Islands, had agencies.

In some states, creating an arts council or commission and supporting it with state money have not gone hand in hand. In 1980, several state arts councils relied exclusively on federal arts dollars to fund their constituencies.

Overall, however, state arts funding has grown dramatically. As the chart below indicates, state funding in 1965 totalled $1.9 million. For the 1981 fiscal year, that amount had grown to $111.7 million.

Yet, even today in many states, the arts agency's position, for several reasons, remains one of the most vulnerable in state government.

First, the arts agency and its staff must contend with a politically sensitive governor and legislature. To be successful, the agency's programs must maintain their artistic purposes while being justified in the more traditional educational, social, and economic terms of other government entities.

The arts agency must communicate successfully with the governor and particularly with the legislature. Arts Task Force members discussed state arts agencies at several of their meetings, and stressed the importance of communication and partnership between the legislature and the arts agency. North Carolina Representative Martin Lancaster, who not only is a member of the state legislature but also chairs the state's Arts Council, said it well:

"One way in which we [Arts Council members] try to communicate and to build trust with the legislature is to let each legislator know exactly where the arts money that they have appropriated is going in their district. What legislators can do to build trust with the arts council is once again to communicate, to let the arts council know what policy direction the state is taking, to involve the arts council in establishing those policies and priorities, and to just become a team working together . . . The most important thing in building trust between the legislature and the council is having a responsible and well respected executive director who has credibility with the legislature and who can walk into a legislator's office, sit down and discuss an issue or a problem, and the legislator will know that he or she knows what they are talking about and will do the right thing."

Second, the arts council members and staff must be sensitive to public needs. To gain budget approval from the executive and legislative branches, most, if not all, of the agency's programs must contain a public service component. The programs must either expand public arts participation in general, provide arts services to a particular needy underserved segment of the public, or further the quality of arts experiences

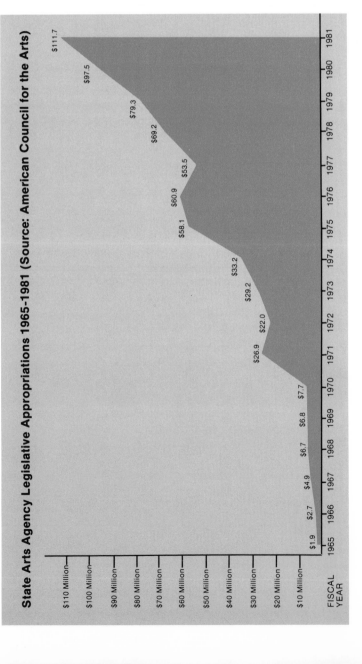

State Arts Agency Legislative Appropriations 1965-1981 (Source: American Council for the Arts)

$111.7 (1981)
$97.5 (1980)
$79.3
$69.2
$53.5
$60.9
$58.1
$33.2
$29.2
$22.0
$26.9
$7.7
$6.8
$6.7
$4.9
$2.7
$1.9 (1965)

FISCAL YEAR: 1965 1966 1967 1968 1969 1970 1971 1972 1973 1974 1975 1976 1977 1978 1979 1980 1981

$110 Million
$100 Million
$90 Million
$80 Million
$70 Million
$60 Million
$50 Million
$40 Million
$30 Million
$20 Million
$10 Million

available to the public.

Third, the agency must balance competing interests within the arts community and try to serve its many divergent constituencies.

Many state arts agencies created in the 1960's responded to the needs of existing arts organizations. Some quickly expanded their roles and developed new programs designed to make the arts accessible to underserved constituencies — rural communities, minority populations, the elderly and disabled, and the young. In making this policy shift, the agencies sometimes alienated their state's major cultural institutions and the legislators who supported those institutions.

"While the National Endowment [for the Arts] has focused on funding the arts where they are, the state arts councils have been left with the responsibility of developing the arts where they are not."
— Roy Helms, former Executive Director, National Assembly of State Arts Agencies

To partially resolve this controversy, many legislatures and arts agencies cooperatively established grant program categories restricted to the state's prominent cultural institutions, with eligible institutions competing for a specific pot of money.

To ensure that every corner of the state receives some state funding, some state agencies allocate a portion of their budgets on a formula basis to a local arts agency in each county. The local agency then distributes the money based on a local plan. This process, commonly called decentralization, places funding decisions with citizens who are more in tune with local cultural needs and priorities.

Decentralization may also help state arts dollars reach more artists, arts organizations, and audiences and may facilitate the discovery of talent. However, decentralization programs have been criticized because they do not ensure adequate state funding for major cultural organizations and because they do not insulate the decision-making process from local politics.

Clearly, state arts agencies need a variety of programs to meet different needs. Happily, many agencies, with cooperation from their state legislatures, are moving in that direction. The chart on the following pages shows the variety of programs offered by state agencies for the 1980 fiscal year.

While the individual agencies vary greatly in their approaches, the chart points out that most state agencies fund prominent and developing arts organizations, touring programs, and local arts councils, and offer newsletters, technical assistance, and other services to the state arts community. However, it also highlights another controversial issue that most state arts agencies face — providing adequate support to individual artists.

Most state funding directed to individual artists is through artists-in-residence programs, which exist in every jurisdiction.[1] These often exemplary programs do reach people underserved by, or in special need of, the arts, including school children, rural and senior citizens, and individuals who are disabled, hospitalized, or incarcerated. They also provide meaningful employment for limited numbers of each state's artists. Often, however, the residencies are neither designed nor intended to facilitate the artist's aesthetic growth. The programs, therefore, should not be seen as a single solution to needed support for artists.

Presently, only 31 jurisdictions offer direct funding to their artists. (Some states are prevented by statute or their constitution from offering direct support to individuals, although this prohibition has been overcome in several instances.) With the chronic inability of visual, performing, and literary artists to find adequate employment in the arts,[2] direct support is expected to be a burning arts issue during the 1980's.

"The creative individual in our society is generally neither encouraged nor rewarded for his efforts. We do not have a climate which encourages experimentation in the arts as we encourage research in science."
— Roy Helms

Two other issues facing state arts agencies are: (1) how best to conduct pre-grant screening of applicants and post-grant evaluation of grantees without becoming bureaucratic mazes spending large percentages of funding on administration at the expense of the individuals and organizations that they are trying to aid and (2) how to deal with a prevailing attitude among grantees that once they receive state arts funding, they become entitled to rely on continued funding in future years.

During the 1970's the state arts agency has had to adapt quickly to growing and changing demands. The agencies will face new challenges in the 1980's.

NOTES
1. The Arts Task Force has included artists-in-residence programs among its recommended legislation. See pages 45-46.
2. For further discussion, see *Artist's Employment and Unemployment,* pages 94-95.

SURVEY OF 1980 STATE ARTS AGENCY PROGRAMS

Programs (columns):

- Artists in Schools Program
- Artists in Communities Program
- Artists in Social Institutions Program
- Major/Prominent Arts Organization Program
- Grants to Visual Artists/Designers/Craftspeople
- Grants to Writers/Poets
- Grants to Musicians/Vocalists/Composers
- Grants to Dancers/Choreographers
- Grants to Actors/Playwrights
- Grants to Film/Video Artists
- Programs Funding Master Artists/Apprentices
- Dance Touring
- Theatre Touring
- Music Touring
- Literary Arts Touring
- Visual Arts Touring
- Artmobile Touring
- Newsletter and Other Publications
- Registry of the State's Artists
- Operates/Funds Technical Assistance Programs to Artists/Organizations Artistically & Administratively
- Funding to Support Local Arts Councils
- Funding to Support Nonprofit Arts Organizations
- Funding to Help Local Governmental/Nonprofit Organizations Expand Services and Public Participation in the Arts
- Sponsorship of Contests with Cash Prizes
- Arts Education Programs Other Than Artists in Schools
- Funds Programs or Services Directed Towards Special Constituencies, Such As Minorities and the Disabled
- Affiliated with a Nonprofit Arts Foundation
- Operate/Affiliated With/Fund A Volunteer Lawyers Association
- Operate/Affiliated With a Business Arts Committee

States (rows): Alabama, Alaska, Arizona, Arkansas, California, Colorado, Connecticut, Delaware, Florida, Georgia, Guam, Hawaii, Idaho, Illinois, Indiana, Iowa, Kansas, Kentucky, Louisiana, Maine, Maryland, Massachusetts, Michigan, Minnesota, Mississippi, Missouri, Montana

⬤ = Funded and/or administered by other than the state arts agency

COMMUNITY ARTS AGENCIES

Ten years ago approximately 200 community arts agencies existed in the United States. Today there are 2,000. Community arts agencies successfully respond to public arts needs as well as serve professional artists, arts institutions, non-traditional arts groups, and non-professional artists. Most community arts agencies have been established through local initiative, because people wanted arts programs in their own communities.

"Community art agencies are making things happen.

"In Bassett, Nebraska (population 900), 1,000 persons attended a November performance of the 'Christmas Carol.' The local council has sponsored artists in residence, concerts, and created a program of public awareness that has motivated impressive local support.

"The Arts Council of San Antonio, Texas has played a major role in the planning, research, and implementation of the major restoration and arts boom that is occurring in that city.

"The Cultural Resources Council of Syracuse and Onondaga County spent ten years in the research, planning and implementation that culminated in the construction and opening of the Civic Center, a performing arts center that serves central New York. The Council now acts as management for that facility. In addition, it provides services to the community and the arts community of Syracuse and Onondaga County.

— *Lee Howard, President, National Assembly of Community Arts Agencies*

State	No. of States With a 1980 Program
New Hampshire	52
New Jersey	42
New Mexico	35
New York	44
North Carolina	29
North Dakota	28
Ohio	29
Oklahoma	25
Oregon	23
Pennsylvania	24
Puerto Rico	8
Rhode Island	49
South Carolina	43
South Dakota	45
Tennessee	28
Texas	38
Utah	13
Vermont	49
Virginia	29
Washington	50
West Virginia	48
Wisconsin	45
Wyoming	43
	9
	24
	37
	13
	20
	12

Each community arts agency is concerned about the cultural needs of its distinct community.

"The purpose of community arts agencies is mainstreaming the arts into all areas of the community — working with seniors, in the schools, with redevelopment, among many other areas ... Community arts agencies can be catalysts for new approaches to problems in urban and rural areas."
— Carl Sautter, former Director, Pasadena (California) Community Arts Center

There are three basic structures among the 2,000 agencies. Approximately 440 are public agencies, part of city or county government, either an arts commission or an arts department or office. About 1,280 are private, nonprofit corporations. The remaining 280 are private, nonprofit agencies that local government officially designates as the city or county community arts agency.

Approximately 70% of the agencies' financial support comes from public and private local sources; regional and state arts agencies together provide about 17%; federal sources, principally CETA funds, provide about 12%.

State legislatures are indirectly involved with community arts agencies through approval of state arts agency appropriations. Many state arts agencies give operational and program support to the local agencies, helping them meet administrative expenses, employ artists in residence, bring in touring groups, or set up community art exhibits. Some state arts agencies fund per capita arts support on a county-by-county or other formula basis. Others supply technical assistance to communities through newsletters, conferences and workshops, and/or a community development representative. In about 15 states, the state agency provides support for an assembly or association of community arts agencies.

The 1980's will see increasing decentralization of government arts support with greater federal and state arts dollars directed to community arts agencies for allocation at the local level.

Legislative approval of state arts funding for community arts agencies is a recognition that the arts are essential to community life, that community cultural planning can effectively assess needs and develop cultural goals, and that a state-local partnership will nurture a climate in which the arts can thrive.

"Where strong local arts agencies exist, good things are happening, not by chance, but because long range goals and objectives have been set, and solid decisions based on thorough knowledge of local needs and resources are being made. This process is fundamental to ensuring accessibility to quality arts at the local level, and after all, whether it's a large urban area, suburban, or rural, arts do happen at the local level."
— Lee Howard

RURAL AREAS AND THE ARTS

Over the past decade the arts have thrived in rural communities. People living in rural areas are developing arts programs and bringing high quality professional artists and nationally known arts companies to their communities.

The traditional arts isolation that rural areas have suffered is disappearing as modern travel opportunities, arts periodicals, and government-supported public television, touring, and artists' residency programs make the arts accessible to rural citizens.

One significant factor affecting the growth of the arts in rural locales is the increase during the last ten years in the number of arts councils serving populations of less than 30,000. Like community agencies in metropolitan areas, these rural agencies help identify and support local artists and encourage people to participate in and experience the arts. In Fredonia, Kansas, for example, the arts council has invited people to retrieve their violins, trumpets, cellos, and saxaphones from their attics and to form a community orchestra. They play to a standing-room-only audience twice a year. Attendance in 1979 at these two concerts, and at the dozens of other activities that the Fredonia Arts Council sponsors, totalled over 4,700 — very impressive for a community of 3,500.

Rural residents are also enjoying high quality talent from outside their regions. In Dunning, Nebraska, 1,000 people saw a performance by the New York-based Raymond Johnson Dance Company; 900 saw the Norman Luboff Choir; and 925 saw the Country Gazette. A community of 160 people that does not appear on most maps, Dunning is the center for 225 elementary and secondary school children from the surrounding 1,000 square-mile area. Ninety-three percent of the population saw the dance performance, and no one had children in the production!

What can state legislators do to encourage the rural arts movement? Legislators can support outreach programs such as:

● **Visiting artists' residencies** that bring professional artists into a rural area to provide performances and classroom instruction, and to develop folk arts and other arts programs.

"One of the most significant programs that we have had is the Community Artists Residency Training (CART) Program. This is a great way to develop the arts at the local level, and in my community it is working beautifully. For the ten towns in my parish, all with populations ranging from less than 500 to under 5,000, we have a resident artist, an opera singer, who is completing a series of performances, one in each town. It's amazing how well this program has worked, how much interest in the arts it has created in each town."

—William Jones, Director, Arts and Humanities Council of Avoyelles Parish, Louisiana

● **Touring programs** in the performing, visual, and literary arts. Some states require state institutions or major nonprofit companies to tour as a condition of receiving state funding. Although these outreach programs are expensive, major institutions can feasibly send smaller ensembles on tour to outlying communities.

● **The funding of rural agencies' programs and staff.**

"A little can go a long way in a rural community. As state legislators approving funding for rural arts, you may never know what a fantastic thing you have done for people in outlying communities of your state."

—Mary Kate Tews, Community Arts Development Consultant and Former Director, New Orleans Recreation Department

● **Per-capita arts funding** to ensure that arts programs are available in rural areas. A few state legislatures require state arts councils to allocate **a portion** of state funding on a per-capita basis to each county. New York and North Carolina are notable examples. However, successful per-capita programs require careful planning and implementation.

Individual legislators can also provide important moral support to rural arts organizations in their districts. A legislator's interest in the state's arts budget is important, and his or her attendance at events is a big boost to morale.

FOLK ARTS AND FOLKLIFE PROGRAMS

The steady growth of state folk arts and folklife programs has been a little-noticed but important recent development. **In the late 1960's Pennsylvania appointed the first 'state folklorist,'** who was affiliated with the Pennsylvania Historical and Museum Commission, and in the early 1970's the Maryland Arts Council included a state folklorist among its staff. In the mid-1970's, with National Endowment for the Arts support, other states began hiring folk arts and folklife coordinators, usually within the state arts agency.

The movement was further stimulated in 1976 by federal legislation creating the American Folklife Center at the Library of Congress.[1] At least three states, Florida, Minnesota, and Montana, have since enacted state legislation modeled after the federal law.[2] **As of 1980, approximately half the states have a formal commitment to folk culture** that has taken various forms ranging from a single-person folk arts coordinator to multi-faceted folklife programs with statutory authority.

Although folk arts and folklife programs are as varied as the states they serve, common characteristics are emerging. Nearly all are handled by a professional folklorist with training in and knowledge of American folk cultural traditions. The programs encourage broad public appreciation of and participation in living state folk cultural traditions. Many make grants to organizations and individuals, but most also initiate and operate specific programs. The programs are concerned with artistic expression, and typically also address not only the arts but also the broader regional, ethnic, and occupational traditions from which those arts arise. Hence, "folklife" sometimes replaces "folk arts" as the preferred program description term.

Among the typical activities fostered by state folklife programs are: community and state folk festivals and folk arts exhibits; folk artists and folklore curricula in schools; production and distribution of books, periodicals, recordings, films, and television programs documenting state folklife, folk arts, and ethnic traditions; field research to locate living resources for use in future programming; folk culture programs in state parks; and grants to community arts councils to develop local folk programs.

State legislators can assist in developing these programs by: enacting legislation establishing folk arts and folklife programs and defining their purpose; amending state arts agency enabling acts to authorize folk arts or folklife programs and supporting budget requests for these programs; and creating a state folklorist when undertaking a reorganization of existing cultural agencies. Folk arts and folklife should be considered as part of the total cultural programming offered by a state to its citizens.

NOTES:
1. *United States Codes Annotated,* Title 20, Section 2103. More recently, the National Endowment for the Humanities has taken an interest in fostering this network, and the Heritage Conservation and Recreation Service within the Department of the Interior has also begun to show interest.
2. *Florida Statutes Annotated,* Sections 265.135-265.138; *Minnesota Statutes Annotated,* Sections 138.81-138.87; and *Montana Codes Annotated,* Sections 22-2-201 to 22-2-205.

FESTIVALS

As citizens, community and business leaders, and government officials have recognized the value of arts festivals, the number of such events has increased dramatically until **now more than 1,000 are held annually.**

Members of the Arts Task Force had the privilege of meeting with prominent officials of the Spoleto Festival, U.S.A., including festival founder and artistic director Gian Carlo Menotti, at a May, 1980 conference in the festival's home city, Charleston, South Carolina. From that meeting as well as other discussions, the Task Force has learned:

● Arts festivals involve broad and often diverse segments of the community working together to give the arts a prominent role in community life.

"People think that art is something that they have to have after dinner. I don't want the artist to be the after dinner mint. I want him to be part of the main meal. And that is why I started Spoleto. I wanted art to be part of the whole community."
— *Gian Carlo Menotti*

"I consider the Spoleto Festival to be a partnership, a partnership that is made up of arts organizations and community, state, federal and private individuals interested in the arts and trying to raise the cultural level of our population.
—*Dr. Theodore Stern, Chairman of the Board of Spoleto, U.S.A.*

● As a result of festivals, new local arts organizations emerge and existing organizations and programs expand.

"As a result of the Prescott Park Festival, there are now 11 arts groups in this little town of 25,000. There are three dance companies, a chamber group, a mime troupe, a visual artists consortium, and others."
— *Jon Kimball, Director, Prescott Park Festival, Portsmouth, New Hampshire*

"The Spoleto Festival has certainly had an impact on all phases of the arts community in Charleston. The Charleston Symphony, which used to be a community orchestra, now has a core of full-time, professional players."
— *Ellen Dressler, Director, Cultural Affairs Division, City of Charleston, and Director of Piccolo Spoleto*

"It was my good fortune to serve as president of Charleston College. Prior to the Spoleto Festival, instruction in the arts was very limited. We had three part-time instructors and about 23 students taking arts classes . . . Today, we have something like 3,800 students taking arts courses and at least 23 full-time arts professors. And I do believe that one reason for this success was the marriage or the relationship of the college and the community and the festival."
— *Theodore Stern*

● Festivals offer a variety of artforms to established and new audiences.

"The Piccolo Spoleto has a different chamber music concert every afternoon. Each free performance is held not only in the regular location but then that same program will be taken out into the poorer sections of our community and a great effort is made to get people there and to give them an opportunity to taste the great beauty of the arts."
— *Charleston Mayor Joseph Riley*

"This is a comprehensive festival, a festival of all the arts."
— *Theodore Stern*

● Fairs and festivals provide a fertile ground for development of new artistic talent.

"It's an opportunity for young people to get recognized. We not only have name artists, but we also have artists that we believe will be some of the great performers of the future. Spoleto is the development of human resources."
— *Theodore Stern*

"The public has been trained to look for 'sacred cows'. . . . It is very important to train the audiences to be creative. They should discover the future sacred cows. 'They are coming to give and they will be responsible for the next great artist.' When you give that feeling to your audience, you'll find that the audience changes and becomes very, very alive."
— *Gian Carlo Menotti*

- Arts festivals have a substantial economic impact on a locale and can revitalize decaying areas and give a community a new identity and focus.

"Last year's Prescott Park Festival played to 250,000 people. This is in a town of 25,000. The money that is generated back into the economy of this small town is in excess of $3 million each year. What this has done in terms of the city fathers and merchants and corporations and businessmen is that they have become very aware that the arts are important to their business, that they make a lot of money from the people attending festival events . . . Emotionally, what the festival has done to our town and to our region — it's given Portsmouth an identification, it's given the people of the city something to be extremely proud of. Portsmouth used to be a town that people drove past to get up to Maine. Now it's a city that has a very thriving tourist trade."

— Jon Kimball

"The Department of Parks, Recreation, and Tourism estimates that Spoleto is responsible for $25 million worth of business to the state during the festival period. That's for an investment by government of about $200,000. I think you would say as a businessman, 'if I can invest $200,000 and generate $25 million in business, that wouldn't be a bad investment at all.'"

— Theodore Stern

"The Saratoga Performing Arts Festival has revitalized a dying community. Thousands of tourists come from as far away as Europe each week during the season."

— New York Assemblyman William Passannante

- Festivals take the arts away from traditional settings, encouraging more people to attend. Exposing additional people to the arts promotes community understanding as well as future arts patronage.

"South Dakota's Prairie Fort State Park was just a number of beautiful old stone buildings and a parade ground. Some of us decided we would try to get a grant to make it come alive with pageantry, art, crafts, musketeers, the whole works. Before the festival, the park was visited by a total of 30,000 people in an entire summer. In June, 1980, we had 33,000 for the festival weekend. For a sparsely populated state, that's good.

— South Dakota Senator Peg Lamont

"The arts, by their very nature, have a great deal of dignity to them. If they're of good quality. When you have senior citizens and young people, and people from all different walks of life and all different economic strata seated together focusing on an arts event, there's a communication that happens among the audience. They respect what you are doing, and that respect often dictates the way they behave. And we've not had any kind of behavior problems."

— Theodore Stern

- An international festival broadens the public's awareness of other cultures.

— Theodore Stern

"Something that I think is very important for all festivals in America is to make them international festivals. So many artistic endeavors are purely local, purely only American. It has been so important for people here [in Charleston] to have in their homes a young Italian pianist, a French violinist, people who do not even speak a word of English. It's marvelous because it helps to create some understanding in this terrible and difficult world . . . It is this wonderful mixture of people from all over the world that really makes this festival very meaningful."

— Gian Carlo Menotti

Festivals are often dependent on partial funding through state arts agency grants or, less frequently, state budget line items. With the demonstrated beneficial impact festivals have, states should consider funding well-organized, broadly based festival events.

MINORITIES AND THE ARTS

The cultural diversity of America's minority communities is one of the nation's greatest assets. These communities contain a rich mixture of language, custom, music, and art that enlivens neighborhood activities and preserves the heritage of the many cultural groups.

Many states have created programs that promote minority cultural activities. The Ohio Arts Council established the Minority Arts Development Program to fund organizations promoting Appalachian, Black, Hispanic, Native American, and Oriental/Asian arts. Hawaii operates an Ethnic Heritage and Humanities Program. This program's purpose is to perpetuate the cultural heritage of the state's many ethnic groups. Ethnic groups that have not organized to perpetuate their heritage are encouraged to do so.

Alabama, Alaska, Arizona, California, Colorado, Minnesota, New Mexico, Oklahoma, and South Dakota have enacted statutes to protect the authenticity of Native American arts and crafts sold within that state. The most effective statute seems to be Alaska's requiring that Native handicrafts made and sold in the state bear an official seal of authenticity issued by the seller with

The Brooklyn Arts & Cultural Association presents performances of traditional dances.

state approval through the Commissioner of Commerce.

Neighborhood arts centers play an important role in bringing minorities and the arts together, providing an opportunity for local residents to engage in art, music, dance, and theatre. Many state arts councils provide funding for these organizations. One such center is the Watts Tower Arts Center in Los Angeles that offers local residents arts classes, poetry readings, music performances, gallery space, and a jazz festival. The arts center activities offer an alternative to television and a chance for local people to form networks among their neighbors to promote their cultural heritage.

For many years Black musicians have struggled to achieve recognition for jazz as an artform. Now fifteen states plus the Virgin Islands are participating in the National Endowment for the Arts' (NEA) Jazz Artists-in-Schools Program, which places jazz artists in neighborhood public schools. The states involved in the program are Illinois, Indiana, Iowa, Kentucky, Louisiana, Maine, Michigan, Montana, Nebraska, New Jersey, North Carolina, Pennsylvania, Tennessee, Texas, and Wisconsin. The NEA's $200,000 program budget is matched by state and local funds.

The twenty-seven jazz artists who participated in the program in 1980 used an interdisciplinary approach to reach over 40,000 children in twenty-nine sites. In order to encourage greater self-expression among the students, some musicians improvised compositions while their listeners sketched lines and shapes to follow the music. Several history classes explored the historical significance of jazz.

One musician even played for a typing class. He emphasized jazz as a rhythmic experience and pointed out the similarities between musical and typing rhythms. In its efforts to carry jazz to an even greater audience, the NEA also administers a $1.3 million jazz program that funds community jazz festivals, workshops, apprenticeships, and an oral history program at the Rutgers Jazz Institute.

One of the most successful arts programs primarily for minority children is the Dance Theatre of Harlem. The Theatre originated as a summer project involving thirty children and two dancers and has grown to over 1,500 students coming from all over the world. The students study academic subjects in the morning and dance, music, or voice in the afternoon. From its modest beginning, the Dance Theatre has evolved into an internationally recognized teaching school and performing company.

These programs represent only a few of the minority artistic activities. This report cannot do more than touch the surface of this expanding cultural area. In all likelihood, this movement will continue to expand during the 1980's.

ARTS AND THE DISABLED

In 1973, Congress passed the Rehabilitation Act, Section 504 of which reads:

No otherwise qualified handicapped person in the United States . . . shall, solely by reason of his handicap be excluded from participating in, be denied the benefits of, or be subjected to discrimination under any program or activity receiving federal financial assistance.

This law, more than any other, has helped "mainstream" disabled individuals into all areas of our society. The arts are no exception.

The arts can enrich the lives of disabled people, and state legislators can play a major role in the mainstreaming process.

"I met with a group of the blind in Maryland just before coming here, and they told me to be sure to mention not to do tokenism. For a while, there has been a move to create sculptural touch gardens for the blind. They want regular gardens to go to and not these disciplining factors you can have to give someone young direction."

". . . it started to get kids off the street and involved. I had been taught I'd never be a dancer and I don't believe in telling people what you can't do, because if there's opportunity and a will, there's a way . . . [T]he arts are one of the most

— Arthur Mitchell, Artistic Director, Dance Theatre of Harlem

One special need of the disabled is arts education. The arts offer an educational, therapeutic, and career-training medium far superior to any other available from which the developmentally disabled and other handicapped children can learn. Nevertheless, in most schools arts education is not being utilized to teach disabled children. As of 1978, only 12% of disabled children enrolled in public schools received any arts training, and for those few the arts were more often an isolated experience rather than a vital and central curriculum component.[1] The National Committee, Arts for the Handicapped, offers these points, among others, supporting arts education for the handicapped:

- Handicapped children achieve in cognitive, affective and aesthetic skills as a result of arts activities.

- The arts are alternative learning approaches for children whose problems interfere with their adjustment to more traditional classroom situations.

- Arts education can be paramount in helping handicapped individuals to use leisure time effectively and to avoid loneliness and social isolation.

- Programs in the arts can be potent vehicles for integrating handicapped individuals and with non-handicapped individuals and

- breaking down barriers of fear and discrimination.

- The arts can be a medium of communication and of stimulating experiences for children with sensory impairments.

- Arts activities can reveal the conflicts and tensions of children with behavioral and emotional problems, and can enable teachers and parents to deal with them in a more understanding way.

- Creative arts can contribute to a positive self-image and greater confidence in children.[2]

How can state legislators help? First, by making sure that each state's special education programs have a meaningful arts component. Second, by providing preservice and inservice training to teach arts educators to work with the physically and mentally disabled and to dispel the preconceived idea that disabled people are less talented and cannot benefit from arts instruction.

Accessibility is a prerequisite for the disabled to enjoy and participate in arts experiences. Under the National Endowment for the Arts' Section 504 regulations, museums and performing arts institutions are making architectural modifications to meet the federal standard of providing reasonable accommodation to the disabled. Reasonable accommodation does **not** require total accessibility. For example, some museums are reorganizing their collections to provide the physically disabled access to representative samplings of all collections without having to make expensive architectural modifications. Many of these institutions are enlisting the assistance of the disabled community to ensure practical modifications.

"Once you have to be lifted up to get into an arts performance or exhibit, you know you are a second-class citizen."
— Ronald Egherman, Deputy Director, University Art Museum, Berkeley

Financial and social accessibility are also important. If the arts are not affordable, if the institutions' staffs are not sensitive to special needs, and if they do not make disabled individuals feel welcome, physical accessibility will be meaningless.

Increasingly ticket voucher programs are making the arts available to the disabled, and institutions are educating and retraining staff members as part of the total accessibility process.

Museums are preparing tours and galleries for the blind that are also open to the general public; they are providing braille markers near the art, cassette tapes explaining exhibits, and readable signs for the visually impaired. Theatre companies are offering readable program notes and narration for the blind, and providing interpreters and special sound systems for the hearing impaired.

NOTES
1. Judy Smith and Wendy Parks, *Humanism and the Arts in Special Education*, Washington, The National Committee, Arts for the Handicapped (September 1978) at 4.
2. *Ibid.*, at 4-5.

THE ARTS' HEALING ROLE

The arts play an important role in the lives

As the above mural indicates, arts therapy and education offer opportunities for individual expression by disabled persons.

NOTES:

1. See, for example, Project SCAMP, Senior Citizens Adventures-in-Music Program, conducted by the Wilmington Music School of Wilmington, Delaware.

2. This study was directed by Hospital Audiences, Inc., of New York City and the Department of Geriatrics Research of The New York State Psychiatric Institute/Columbia University. Dr. Robert Shomer was the project director.

ARTISTS' EMPLOYMENT AND UNEMPLOYMENT

Artists have the highest unemployment rate among professional and technical workers. A 1976 study of Massachusetts visual artists' employment found 12.5% unemployed, but two-thirds of those employed had only part-time positions; 68.5% received less than $1,000 from the sale of their artwork, and only 4.4% earned more than $7,000 from their sales.[1]

"Less than 2% of the artists in this country are able to support themselves by the sale of their art alone."

— Ron Blumberg, Founder and past president, Artists for Economic Action, Los Angeles

Among performing artists, the statistics are even worse. In 1976 a U.S. Department of Labor funded AFL-CIO study of five major performing artists' unions found that only about one-third of the members in the five

---

The arts provide a means of communication for the elderly who have lost verbal or motor skills. Arthritic patients regain the use of stiff fingers by constant practice on an organ or piano during music therapy classes.[1] Stroke victims receive arts therapy as a form of rehabilitation, and can make sense of life by creatively expressing past joys and sorrows. Through art or music, they can relive happy moments, sort out thoughts about the present, and prepare for the future.

Research indicates that programs have an "activating result" on participants in nursing home programs, stimulating them generally and causing them to become involved in other non-arts programs.[2]

The arts help counteract the physically sterile and often hostile and tense prison environment by offering a creative outlet, providing vocational training, and encouraging individuality and self-expression. Prison artists are highly respected, and the arts in addition transcend language and education barriers.

Arts therapy is also used to help the mentally ill. For patients who have repressed their feelings or lost their grip on reality, the simple task of putting brush to paper may unleash a torrent of emotion. Similarly, dance therapy uses the art of movement to integrate the body and emotions in self-expression. It also constructively channels physical energy that might otherwise be directed toward self-destruction.

Ultimately, all individuals whose lives are touched by the arts benefit from the positive influence of the creative experience.

---

of society's disadvantaged members. Participation in the arts brightens the lives of the institutionalized elderly, emotionally disturbed, and incarcerated by helping ease the boredom and loneliness that too often accompany their lives.

The arts serve as a form of habilitation — that is, they can aid people in living productive and enjoyable lives. This role is vitally important to the mentally and physically handicapped, for arts therapy improves their physical capabilities and relieves the emotional stress caused by their disabilities. Nowhere is this fact more evident than with children unable to master verbal communication. By drawing, children express in a nonverbal manner the ideas, thoughts, and emotions that they find difficult and sometimes frightening to express verbally. Similarly, children who have failed in reading and arithmetic need not suffer the same frustration in arts classes. There is no right or wrong in the arts — only individual expression.

Whether children are average, gifted, or handicapped, music will teach them listening skills, a learning fundamental. The musical arts are also one of the few areas of learning in which children may express themselves emotionally rather than verbally. As children listen to music, they discover rhythm, develop coordination, and are free to express joy by singing, dancing, or playacting to the sound.

The institutionalized elderly also find a means of self-expression in arts experiences. Involvement in amateur dramatic productions brings new skills, new friends, and new challenges and prevents the disorientation and depression of too much unstructured leisure time.

unions worked full-time in arts jobs. Among other findings: Only 20% worked for one employer, and between 10% and 20% worked for ten or more different employers in one year; half the members held jobs unrelated to their profession; **although half had completed at least four years of college, their median income was markedly below that attained by other professional groups with an equivalent high level of education;** and performing artists had a higher proportion of, longer, and more frequent periods of unemployment than did other workers.[2]

"At any given time, 85% of our actors are unemployed. The average Actors Equity member in 1977 made under $3,000."
— Michael Fox, Actors Equity Association

According to the federal Bureau of Labor Statistics, the total number of visual, performing, and literary artists increased 44% during the 1970's; at the end of 1979, there were 1,304,000 artists in this country. However, during the last half of that decade, the number of musicians declined, from 165,000 in 1976 to 154,000 in 1979.[3]

Artists' unemployment problems are compounded by their frequent ineligibility for unemployment insurance benefits. The AFL-CIO study reported that from 40% to 60% of the performing artists who were unemployed did not collect any unemployment compensation during the time they were out of work. Because they frequently work simultaneously but intermittently for several different employers, they may be ineligible because unemployment insurance liability attaches only to a single employer. Artists registering in their profession may also be disqualified as self-employed individuals not available for work.

State legislatures may want to consider revising unemployment insurance laws and regulations to accommodate artists' nontraditional working patterns. One possible solution is to qualify artists solely on an earnings test, irrespective of their duration of employment.

A tremendous boon to artists' employment in the last half of the 1970's was the federal Comprehensive Employment and Training Act (CETA). As of 1979, the Department of Labor was supporting CETA/Arts programs at about $200 million annually, $50 million more than the National Endowment for the Arts' total funding! CETA helped emerging artists prepare for professional status through employment and training that, at the same time, provided cultural and other public services to the community.

State art agencies were actively involved in applying for and administering CETA/Arts programs. The Vermont Council on the Arts, for example, perceived a significant need in the state's human service institutions for recreational leaders, arts coordinators, and arts therapists. Between 1975 and 1980 the Council utilized over 400 artists who were responsible for placing themselves in work sites and negotiating contracts with human service agencies. This strategy provided the artists with the skills to secure future employment.

State arts agencies also directly and indirectly employ artists through their various grants programs. In 31 states, artists are awarded direct grants or fellowships, some requiring completion of specific projects, others with no obligations attached. Percent-for-art laws in 19 states and Guam offer employment opportunities for visual artists. Grants to institutions and community arts organizations often result in artists' employment.

NOTES:
1. Roosevelt, Rita K., Ph.D., *Career Development: A Profile of Massachusetts Visual Arts*, Boston, The Artists Foundation (1977).

2. *Employment, Underemployment and Unemployment in the Performing Arts: The Results of a Survey of Performing Artists*, Human Resources Development Institute, AFL-CIO (December 1977). Actors continue to suffer an extraordinarily high rate of unemployment — 35.8% at the end of 1979.

3. This and other BLS data are contained in a report, *Employment and Unemployment of Artists in 1979*, compiled by the Research Division, National Endowment for the Arts, and published in February, 1980.

STATE SUPPORT FOR PUBLIC BROADCASTING

State support for public broadcasting has expanded dramatically since 1967 when the organizational framework for a federally funded public broadcasting system was established. During fiscal 1979, forty-six states supported public television broadcasting with total funding of $103,567,838. The South Carolina Legislature gives its public television stations the highest state funding at $10.5 million, a figure which is 75.8% of the network's total tax-supported income. One reason for this exemplary support is that the chairmen of the Legislature's House Ways and Means Committee and Senate Finance Committee sit on the South Carolina

Educational Television Commission. The states with the next largest public television budgets are New York ($9.6 million), Kentucky ($7.3 million), Louisiana ($6.9 million), and Maryland ($5.1 million).

The largest state budgets for public radio include Wisconsin ($1.03 million), New York ($510,235), Florida ($495,793), Alaska ($453,377), and Puerto Rico ($446,832). Alaska public radio's twelve stations receive more than 36% of their income from the state. The network has been instrumental in delivering programs to small communities spread over vast distances, and in many cases is the only radio outlet serving an area.

A 1979 Michigan law allows a state income tax credit rather than a deduction for donations to public TV and radio stations. The law allows a credit of up to $100 per year ($200 for a married couple). The credit is equal to 50% of the donation but may not exceed 20% of the individual's tax liability.

Public broadcasting of the arts is an exciting concept whose time has come. Television provides front row seats for many first-time viewers who will be exposed to the best of opera, ballet, and drama.

"One of the things that television has proven that it can do is develop a new constituency for the arts; it can make programming and the arts accessible to people who simply never would have that opportunity any other way."
— Henry Cauthens, General Manager, South Carolina Educational Television

The Public Broadcasting System (PBS) is creating the Public Subscriber Network, a nonprofit cultural cable television network. PBS will share subscriber revenues with members of the American Arts Alliance, an association of the nation's major arts institutions. PBS will compete with several commercial arts-oriented cable networks.

With government funding, public television and public radio stations have been able to deliver exciting new programs to American audiences. Opera, dance, drama, and children's television are brought to millions of viewers daily. Radio waves carry the sounds of jazz, bluegrass, and symphonies to listeners. These cultural programs are dependent on continued private and public support; the states can continue to provide an important portion of public broadcasting's government funding.

MUSEUMS

Museums play a central role in preserving the cultural, artistic, scientific, and historic heritage of each generation. Millions of visitors passed through the doors of American museums last year.

Sources of museum funding include the Institute of Museum Services (IMS), created by Congress in 1976, which in 1979 awarded over $7 million to museums in all fifty states. For fiscal 1980, Congress increased the Institute's allocation to $10.4 million, 75% of which is for general operating support grants and 25% for special project grants. Several states have discussed establishing an agency modeled on the IMS.

The National Endowment for the Humanities (NEH) also funds museums. History, science, or natural history museums may seek NEH dollars that are distributed in each state by volunteer humanities committees.

Funding for new museums often involves a partnership between state and local interests. In 1980 New Mexico created a state natural history museum. The state legislation establishing the museum required the City of Albuquerque to purchase the land for the museum site and to obtain $2 million in private funds to match the $8 million the state provided from severance tax revenues. To convince other legislators of the importance of a natural history museum, State Senator John Irick, an Arts Task Force member, had sponsored a bill in 1977 to create a paleontological expedition. The results of the expedition were displayed in a state capitol exhibit. The exhibit impressed the legislators with the potential impact of a state natural history museum, and a short time later, Senator Irick's bill creating the museum was passed.

Louisiana, Maine, North Carolina, West Virginia, and New Jersey have created and funded state-administered museums. The New Jersey State Museum in Trenton emphasizes the state's heritage in the fine arts, cultural history, archeology, ethnology, and natural science. The Louisiana State Museum in New Orleans and the Maine State Museum in Augusta concentrate on presenting exhibits that detail their states' histories. The West Virginia State Museum houses exhibits of historical and artistic interest. North Carolina has three state museums devoted to the state's history, art, and natural history. Interestingly, four of the five states with state museums also have cabinet-level cultural departments, indicating a broad state commitment to the arts and culture.